the Midlife Review

A guide to work, wealth and wellbeing

Steve Butler and Tony Watts

RETHINK PRESS

First published in Great Britain in 2020 by
Rethink Press (www.rethinkpress.com)

Cover image © Shutterstock | igor kisselev

Contents

Foreword

Are you old?

According to a recent UK survey,[1] we're quite settled in agreeing that 'youth' ends at thirty. But when are we 'old'? Ask an eighteen-year-old and they will typically say old age is 'from age sixty'. Ask the country as a whole and they will say 'from age seventy'. But ask the seventy-year-old and they will most likely say 'from age eighty'. So, while many who are reading this book may have to accept that 'youth' is behind us, we can all take comfort from the insight that none of us are 'old'.

---

1   YouGov (2018) 'How Young are "Young People"? And At What Age Does A Person Become "Old"?' https://yougov.co.uk/topics/politics/articles-reports/2018/03/06/how-young-are-young-people-and-what-age-does-perso

Age, and ageing, is set to be one of the biggest debates in the decade to come. We will all be challenged to create a society that supports all and empowers all, regardless of the date on our birth certificate.

The media spotlight has already been shone on the views of the 'millennials' and the demands of the 'boomers'. But far less attention has been given to the hopes of the millions lying in between – the 'midlifers'. This must change. And this book brilliantly explains why, with a focus on the workplace.

Age in the workplace is changing, rapidly. Nearly one in three employees are now over the age of fifty. This is our fastest growing employee age group, but we are failing to support this experienced and expert population.

At age fifty, about eight in ten of us are active in the labour market. But as we progress towards our sixties this collapses towards five in ten. By the time we reach our state pension age, most of us have already left the labour market. Incredibly, a man today is exiting the workplace at a younger age on average than he did in 1950, despite his greatly enhanced life expectancy.[2]

---

2   Office Statistics: Department for Work and Pensions (2019) 'Economic Labour Market Status of Individuals Aged 50 And Over, Trends Over Time: September 2019'. www.gov.uk/government/statistics/economic-labour-market-status-of-individuals-aged-50-and-over-trends-over-time-september-2019

For some, this early exit may be through fortunate choice. But for many others, it is being driven by a lack of opportunity and support. In short, the UK is failing its fastest growing, and arguably most valuable, population of workers. If we fail to change our ways, we will all be worse off.

My employer, Aviva, wakes up every morning trying to help society prepare for later life. We help six million people in the UK save for and live in retirement. Yet we recognised that we had more to do to support a fuller working life.

We have more than five thousand employees aged forty-five and over. And each carries an average seventeen years of loyal company service. That's a total of 85,000 years of invaluable experience. Yet one in three told us that they feared age was a barrier to opportunity. For the good of the individual, and the good of Aviva, this had to change. We did this by introducing our own midlife review, and we are now reaping the rewards.

Experience tells me that few business leaders have yet to wake up to this urgent need for change. From my various discussions with Steve Butler, he is clearly one who gets it.

His book positively and powerfully outlines the need to invest in our midlife population. And he does this through the eyes of the employee and the eyes of the employer. Steve has been wise to present the debate from both perspectives. The needs may be different, but I confidently believe that by investing in our growing population of midlife workers, the businesses that choose to do so will grow too. It's a win-win.

Steve Butler is a leading thinker when it comes to age in the workplace; Aviva strives to be a leader; and by reading Steve's words, you can a leader too.

By acting today to ensure that age is no barrier to opportunity, I am confident we are acting to ensure tomorrow's success.

Let's succeed together.

Alistair McQueen
Head of Savings & Retirement, Aviva

Preface

Midlife: a time for businesses and individuals to prepare for the future
by Steve Butler

Recently, I took a month off to go climbing in the Himalayas. After many years working hard, building up a business and raising a family, I decided it was time to get back in touch with myself. You could call it an 'early fiftieth birthday present' as I am rapidly reaching that landmark. I came back refreshed and re-energised, and (thanks to my supportive colleagues) the business had run smoothly without me.

I know I'm not alone: other friends and acquaintances around my age have taken sabbaticals to volunteer, study and to travel, investing in their personal development and taking a mental and physical break from the daily routine before returning to their previous roles. Others have altered direction around this point, retraining or going back to university for a few years to do another degree. Some have changed track completely – going into consultancy or another sector entirely, not least those 'cut loose' by businesses in the financial and legal sectors keen to have a younger workforce.

Once upon a time, reacting in this way may have been called a midlife crisis: an ill-considered move when every sensible person focused on their career. Now this is perceived as a positive response to what is going on around us, rather than a panicked reaction. Many view this as a time when (for better or worse) they can take stock of what lies ahead and set a new course if that is what is needed; and I believe that this mid-career phase of reflection and change is going to become routine, normal and entirely understandable.

Gearing up for the '100-year-life'

The 'working life' timeline is stretching as life expectancy rises and pension provision becomes less generous. The prospect of working for fifty to sixty years will make it ever more difficult to stay on one career trajectory. It is only natural that people working for that long will want to stop, re-evaluate, take time out to pursue other interests, or explore other avenues at some point. The typical structure of our careers looks different to the way it did just a decade or two ago.

Given the choice, many of us will change our roles, work less, and/or take more time to pursue personal passions in our later working years or to care for other family members. Expect less of a straight line (eg study, first job, series of promotions, retirement) and more of a meander (eg study, first job, promotions, go back to study, second career, wind down, become self-employed, semi-retire).

For individuals, this potentially opens up the opportunity for a fuller, richer and more fulfilling life – the old 'cliff edge' retirement a thing of the past, but it also throws up new challenges. How are people going to negotiate changes with their employer or go about finding a new job after retraining in their forties or fifties? How can people finance the years ahead if they are going to work less, retrain or return to study? People's savings patterns may need to change with their priorities: the pot of money they have traditionally accumulated to fund their retirement may get dipped into to sustain a sabbatical, reskilling, or a year out to care for a loved one.

Where, though, does this leave employers? Will this lead to companies experiencing an exodus of talent and experience just as the pipeline of younger people coming through dwindles? Should recruitment strategies change if it becomes normal for people in their forties and fifties to temporarily 'drop out', wind down or retrain? What about retention: how can employers keep their best people under these circumstances? What kinds of skills will they need to give their staff when they are dropping in and out of the workplace and changing careers more frequently?

This book attempts to answer some of the questions from the perspectives of both employee and employer, and it uses as the fulcrum the concept of a 'Midlife Review' (MLR), sometimes referred to as the 'Midlife Career Review' and the 'Midlife MOT': a conscious mechanism to stimulate a conversation between employers and their personnel.

We have used the phrase MLR through this book because it should (ideally) cover all aspects of a person's life – their career is one part of that.

My perspective – and that of an ever-expanding number of companies – is that for employees to take time to reflect on what lies ahead actually presents *them* with an excellent opportunity to prepare for their own future and to maximise the talents of *all* of their employees in a more structured way.

The MLR has been gaining significant traction in recent years. This book includes interviews with some of those who have been actively piloting schemes to the point where the Government itself has recognised the huge part it can play in enabling employers to recruit, retain and retrain the older people they will need on board as the nation's demographics radically shift in the coming decades. Trade unions have also recognised the advantages of an MLR in enabling employees to enjoy a fulfilling and rewarding career in their later working years as well as ensure they have the finances in place to lead a secure and comfortable retirement.

After an introduction on the background of the MLR and an overview of the demographics driving it, the book divides into two parts: the first is for employees and the second provides information and guidance for employers. I would encourage both 'sides' to read and take on board the other's point of view as this is essential for an MLR to achieve its objectives. To date, the work proving its worth has been undertaken primarily by larger organisations, although that is changing. As a company that advises small to mid-size enterprises (SMEs) on their employee benefits, I believe there is huge value to be gained by smaller businesses in adopting the concept.

The mission of this book is to encourage companies of all sizes to look at the benefits of the MLR and is intended to provide a starting point for adopting the process. It follows on from my earlier book *Manage the Gap: Achieving Success With Intergenerational Teams*, which explored the bigger picture of how you motivate and manage different generations of employees within your workforce. It gathers up much of what has been discussed, piloted and researched and adds my own perspective as an employer to the mix as well as the views and experience of my co-writer, Tony Watts OBE, who has spent many years working in this arena. We have also talked to experts in their field on 'encore careers', on making a positive transition to later life and on how wellbeing is at the core of that later life.

There is no right or wrong way to develop an MLR: one of our conclusions (spoiler alert) is that businesses will need to tailor their own, but hopefully this book will encourage companies and employees to start conversations that will lead to precisely that.

'Times change, and so must I...'
by Tony Watts OBE

If you know the source of that quote, congratulations – it was uttered by actor Matt Smith in 2013 when he regenerated as The Doctor in *Doctor Who*.

As I'm someone who really did hide behind the sofa in the earliest days of the programme, you can probably guess my vintage. When I was starting out on my career, the assumed path to success was to get hired by a big company, work your way up and hang on for a decent pension. I tried that but conspicuously failed to fit the mould. I have always been looking for the next challenge, and so my career has been spent precariously flitting from role to role.

That, curiously, has enabled me to navigate my later years as new technologies have emerged to change the way we communicate – if not the guiding principles behind communication. Being able and willing to 'morph' or regenerate (in *Doctor Who* terminology) is also a key message for readers of this book. Whatever changes we have seen in the workplace in the last forty years will be nothing compared with the decades to come. It's impossible to plan for a future that you can't yet envision but you can equip yourself to adapt when the need arises.

I've always loved the concept that one can reinvent oneself and The Doctor has long embodied that – just as my musical hero David Bowie did. Bowie never waited until someone overtook what he was doing: he did that himself. I admire those who recognise that the world is constantly changing and that one should not fear to evolve and embrace that; to be confident that one's core skills and competencies can be updated and refashioned to meet fresh challenges.

Age is not a barrier: business, the arts, literature, and even the world of politics is studded with success stories of those who have adapted to change and renewed their careers often quite late in their lives.

Not that long ago, later life was invariably portrayed as an inexorable descent towards the precipice of retirement, a ceremony accompanied by polite applause for a job well done, golden handshakes and carriage clocks, followed by the retiree tending their allotment and dozing off in front of the television.

Now, for many (if not all), greater longevity and better health in later life opens up a panoply of new and exciting opportunities. To apply skills acquired over a lifetime in new and fulfilling ways. To continue growing and learning new skills, as well as contributing and earning. Why would you stop work if you enjoy what you do? Equally, why would you if you haven't got enough money tucked away for what may be a long retirement? This is an issue facing large numbers of people now in midlife.

These twin drivers for individuals – choice and necessity – are currently coinciding with several imperatives for business and the state: employers need the expertise, energy and experience of older people because fewer young people are entering the workforce, and the state can't support an ever-burgeoning retired population. Simply expressed, UK plc cannot afford to let older people head for the golf course and drive (chip or putt) off into the sunset. The MLR can play a big part here.

I first became acquainted with the concept in its earliest days, in my voluntary role representing older people in Government. I knew it was an incredibly sensible notion whose time would soon come. Enough research has now gone into it to amply demonstrate its value to employers and individuals alike. I hope that the arguments and ideas in this book will inspire you to take the MLR concept forwards in *your* enterprise.

Introduction: What Is The Midlife Review?

Where, then, does the MLR or 'Midlife MOT' fit into the scheme of things? It is not to be confused with the regular reviews which many employers provide – usually looking at how the person's career is progressing, problems to be resolved, their performance over the last period, salary and benefits etc. The MLR is far more focused on the mid- to long-term and will look at a person's situation far more holistically: providing the starting point for reflection on their finances, work aspirations and overall wellbeing. In short, it explores everything that can impact upon a person's work, with a view to developing a clear perspective on what will enable them to be their best for themselves and their employer – which may mean going part-time, changing role, winding down to retirement or even leaving entirely.

The overriding objective is to retain the talents and experience of older people in the workforce by identifying the right course to meet their needs and aspirations.

If you're an employer or manager who simply views their staff as worker bees, readily replaceable when one leaves, then this book probably isn't for you. Its focus is on how you nurture and maximise the asset that each individual represents. Equally, if you're reading this as an employee who simply sees turning up to work as a way to fill the nine-to-five until you can afford to leave, reading how to get the best out of your life over the next ten, twenty or more years might not appeal. However, if you recognise that the world of work is changing – and that the challenges that face both employers and employees can be converted to opportunities, then please read on.

Handled correctly, we believe that the last ten or twenty years of a person's working life can be the most productive – and the most rewarding. It simply requires a recalibration of how employers and employees talk to each other, with both sides understanding the other's perspective in order to plan ahead – together. This shouldn't be a revolutionary concept, especially if you put equal weight on both of the words in the phrase 'human resources'.

Too many experienced and valuable employees are being allowed to leave when it becomes a problem (for a variety of reasons) for them to continue working full-time in their current role, with no efforts being made to find ways to accommodate them. While it's no longer as commonplace as it was a few years ago, too many are actually being incentivised to retire early. Not only does this approach lose the organisation a vast amount of expertise and knowledge, but many of those leaving full-time work at a relatively young age (with possibly thirty or even forty years of life ahead of them) simply aren't prepared for their new situation.

Having infinitely more time for the garden, golf or grandchildren can have a lot of appeal, but it's not for everyone. For some, early retirement can also mean getting by on a fairly limited income – restricting what you can do in the years ahead, especially if one's situation changes. For others, it signals a loss of status and purpose, and possibly isolation and loneliness, that can lead to depression and poor health.

One of the experts in this book talks of 'retiree's regret syndrome', when boredom and the lack of stimulation and company set in – often two years after they leave. This is because retirement has traditionally been seen as a cliff edge: a binary choice between working and not working. It needn't be like this, and the way to change this pattern is by opening up a constructive dialogue between employers and employees on what would work best for both of them. In other words, the MLR.

How demographics have changed the working/retirement narrative

In developed countries, the concept of a 'funded retirement' after a lifetime of study and work is well and truly woven into the warp and weft of what society expects, but what we can look forward to is also rapidly evolving as public health improves and productivity slows.

There was a time when relatively low life expectancy meant that retirement for most working people was fairly brutish and short: it is telling that the UK's first recipients of an 'Old Age Pension' from the state were some 600,000 lucky few who (in January 1909) had managed to reach the grand old age of seventy and were deemed to be 'of good character'.[3]

At that time only one in four people managed to live that long, and the reward for doing so was just five shillings a week (7s/6d for couples): a meagre amount, but potentially preserving them from the terrifying prospect of the workhouse.

Pensions have long been the key to surviving retirement in some degree of comfort and dignity, and they have been around for longer than many people realise. In this country they were first paid to Royal Naval officers (1670) before becoming popular in Victorian times for those in occupations such as the

---

3   'Old Age Pensions, the First Payments', *The Times*, 31 December 1908.

railway (1853) and nursing (1874), followed by similar schemes for civil servants, teachers and the police. It is telling that they were seen as a recruitment tool by organisations like the railway companies competing for skilled and committed staff.

As society enjoyed greater prosperity during the course of the twentieth century, the state pension increased in value, the State Earnings Related Pension Scheme (SERPS) was introduced in 1978, and more employers developed their own pension schemes as a way to attract and retain talented people. The balance tipped significantly in the post-war years as increasingly generous company and public sector pension schemes meant that many individuals found themselves able to retire before state pension age (SPA) – then sixty-five for men and sixty for women.

You don't require a long memory to recall the days when many companies and public sector employers saw fifty or fifty-five as a watershed in an employee's working life. With a raft of younger, upwardly thrusting staff kicking their heels and increasingly expensive final salary pensions coming into view, many took the opportunity to put a whole tier of senior management out to grass.

There were plenty more good people in the pipeline, but that was then – and this is now. The seismic plates have shifted within society and the economy, and we now need to hold onto good people wherever possible, not least because of the high cost of recruiting and training when 'churn' in the workplace is at an all-time high. Radical changes are needed in the light of several inexorable facts: for employers, a tightening pipeline of younger workers coming through; for employees, significantly reduced retirement incomes as final salary pensions are phased out, alongside whatever savings they have needing to stretch further.

Age distribution of the UK population, 1975 to 2045 (projected)

Year	UK Population	0 to 15 years (%)	16 to 64 years (%)	65 years and over (%)
1975	56,226,000	24.9	61.0	14.1
1985	56,554,000	20.7	64.1	15.2
1995	58,025,000	20.7	63.4	15.8
2005	60,413,000	19.3	64.7	15.9
2015	65,110,000	18.8	63.3	17.8
2025	69,444,000	18.9	60.9	20.2
2035	73,044,000	18.1	58.3	23.6
2045	76,055,000	17.7	57.8	24.6

Source: 'Overview of the UK population: March 2017', Office for National Statistics

In July 2014, The UK Commission for Employment and Skills estimated that over twelve million vacancies needed to be filled in the subsequent ten years (mainly because of the retirement of older workers), but with only seven million young people currently in the pipeline to replace them, five million vacancies would remain unfilled.[4]

For many businesses, that predicted skills shortage has already come to pass: according to the 2018 Open University Business Barometer, the overwhelming majority of organisations in the UK (91%) had struggled to find workers with the right skills over the previous twelve months. They estimate that the shortfall is now costing businesses an additional £6.33 billion a year in recruitment fees, inflated salaries, temporary staff and training for workers hired at a lower level than intended.[5]

Data from the Recruitment & Employment Confederation's 'Jobs Outlook' report shows that between May and July 2019, 46% of employers of permanent staff expressed concern about finding enough suitable candidates for hire.[6] Recruiting is particularly problematic in some key sectors (notably finance, teaching and software), locations (London, the South-East and North-West) and (among smaller businesses) at senior management level (Directors and CEOs).[7]

---

4   TUC (2014) 'Representing An Ageing Workforce: Challenges and opportunities for trade unions'. www.tuc.org.uk/sites/default/files/RepresentingAnAgeingWorkforce.pdf
5   The Open University (2018) 'The UK Skills Shortage is Costing Organisations £6.3 Billion'. www.open.ac.uk/business/apprenticeships/blog/uk-skills-shortage-costing-organisations-£63-billion
6   Elizabeth Howlett (2019) 'UK Employers Express Concern Over Shortage of Skilled Candidates', *People Management*. www.peoplemanagement.co.uk/news/articles/uk-employers-concerned-over-shortage-of-skilled-candidates
7   '2020 UK Skills Shortage & Demand By Region'. www.smallbusinessprices.co.uk/uk-skills-shortage

According to a 2017 report in *The Independent* on current trends, the Local Government Association estimates that by 2024 there will be more than four million too few highly skilled people to meet demand for high skilled jobs.[8]

But as one curve goes down, another rises: the increased availability of older people in the general population because of the 'birth bulge' during the fifties and sixties. By a happy coincidence, there are also real incentives for many of this cohort to stay economically active. Greater longevity means that anyone retiring at sixty-five can expect (on average) to live for a further 18.6 years if they are male and 21 years for females.[9] This increasing longevity is having a big impact on pensions incomes and means they have to make any pension pot last much longer than their parents did.

This, combined with other factors in the financial sector, means that anyone taking the safe route and putting their pension pot into an annuity can now expect historically low returns. In 1995, a sixty-five year old man buying a standard 'level' annuity with a £100,000

---

8   Ben Chapman (2017) 'UK skills shortage could cost £90bn per year with Brexit to make things worse, say councils', *Independent*. www.independent.co.uk/news/business/news/uk-skills-shortage-cost-90-billion-brexit-latest-news-lga-local-government-association-a7825061.html
9   Office for National Statistics (2019) 'National Life Tables, UK: 2016 to 2018'. www.ons.gov.uk/peoplepopulationandcommunity/birthsdeathsandmarriages/lifeexpectancies/bulletins/nationallifetablesunitedkingdom/2016to2018

pension pot could have typically expected to draw an annual income of £11,100. In September 2010 the figure stood at £6,060. Today, it is £4,100.[10]

Research recently published on the comparison website MoneySuperMarket.com amply demonstrates just how few of us are really prepared for retirement or know how much we need to afford to live it comfortably: the annual income figure typically deemed 'sufficient' in retirement to lead a no-frill lifestyle is £26,000.[11] Bearing in mind that a full new state pension in 2019/20, based on thirty-five years of contributions, is £168.60 a week (£8,767.20 a year),[12] that involves making up a shortfall of over £17,000 from a private pension – in return requiring a private pension pot of some £370,000 (assuming an approximate yield of 5%).

Worryingly, their research shows that when people are asked to estimate the size of pot they require, the average figure given is £200,915. Even more worrying, the amount actually being saved is even smaller: LV='s research reveals that those now aged between forty-five and fifty-four currently have an average pension pot

---

10 Derin Clark (2019) 'Annuity Incomes Fall to Historic Low'. www.moneyfacts.co.uk/news/retirement/annuity-incomes-fall-to-historic-low

11 *HR News* (2018) 'Revealed: The Average Brit Underestimates The Amount They Need To Retire By £169,000'. www.hrnews.co.uk/revealed-the-average-brit-underestimates-the-amount-they-need-to-retire-by-169000

12 GOV.UK Policy Paper (2018) 'Benefit and pension rates 2018 to 2019'. www.gov.uk/government/publications/proposed-benefit-and-pension-rates-2018-to-2019

worth just £71,342.[13] Just as concerning is the pension pot gender disparity: by age fifty, women have saved an average of £56,000 – just half the £112,000 average saved by men.[14] Those planning their retirement are now also having to factor in future care costs as support from councils for those with lower levels of saving is being inexorably sliced back.

As part of their Fuller Working Lives background evidence, the Department of Works and Pensions (DWP) forecasts an estimated twelve million people are heading towards an insufficient retirement income.[15] For employers and employees alike, the solution is the same: to delay retirement and enable older people to remain in the workplace for as long as possible.

The legislative background

Thankfully, the Government woke up to the impending double whammy of a skills shortage plus inadequate pension funding some time ago and have put in place a number of supportive measures.

---

13 LV= (2019) 'State of Retirement 2017: Are you spending enough time planning for retirement?' www.lv.com/pensions-retirement/articles/state-of-retirement-chapter-1

14 FTADVISER (2018) 'Women Aged 50 Have Half Pension Savings of Men'. www.ftadviser.com/retirement-income/2018/01/30/women-aged-50-have-half-pension-savings-of-men

15 Department for Work and Pensions Official Statistics (2014) 'Fuller Working Lives – background evidence'. www.gov.uk/government/statistics/fuller-working-lives-background-evidence

The Employment Equality Age Regulations (2006) prohibited employers from unreasonably discriminating against employees on grounds of age.[16] In 2011, the default retirement age was abolished, preventing employers from compulsorily retiring a member of staff at age sixty-five unless they could objectively justify it, and the mechanisms to make the SPA equal for both men and women at sixty-five by 2019 started to take effect, with a built-in increase to age sixty-six by 2020 (and subsequent plans to raise it from sixty-six to sixty-seven between 2026 and 2028).

The Pension Taxation Act (2014) has also provided extra headroom for anyone looking to adjust their retirement and working plans by allowing individuals to access their pension pots on a more flexible basis from age fifty-five.[17]

With these statutory changes in place, the DWP launched an initiative called 'Fuller Working Lives' in February 2017. As Damian Hinds, Minister of State for Employment, pointed out in the foreword at the time, we are living, on average, almost a decade longer than our grandparents. 'Despite the increased longevity, people today are actually leaving the labour market earlier than in 1950. As well as those having planned and set aside to retire early, there are a lot of people exiting... before ideally they would choose.'

---

16 The Employment Equality (Age) Regulations 2006. www.legislation. gov.uk/uksi/2006/1031/contents/made
17 Taxation of Pensions Act 2014. www.legislation.gov.uk/ ukpga/2014/30/contents/enacted

He goes on to reinforce the message that, for many, this will mean living on an income which will not be enough to maintain the lifestyle they had hoped for. 'Fuller Working Lives: a partnership approach' represents an important milestone in government strategy. As well as highlighting why, as the population ages, employers will need to draw on the skills and experience of older workers to avoid loss of labour, it also looks at how that can be sensibly achieved.

It contains recommendations around flexible working, retraining, self-employment, volunteering and phased retirement. It also waxes lyrical about the strategic benefits of a multi-generational workforce to businesses. Critically, the report also draws attention to the wasted opportunities for individuals, the economy and businesses alike: by the time they reach SPA, one in four men and one in three women have not worked for five years or more. The reasons: essentially a combination of caring responsibilities, wrong skills set and poor physical or mental health.

Part of the reason is historical: there was a time when older workers with health conditions were allowed to get signed off, quietly drop out of the system and receive disability benefits, massaging the unemployment figures and silently recognising that they might never be economically active again. That avenue is now significantly restricted as the Government tightens its criteria around those deemed 'Fit for Work', but still an estimated one million over-fifties who would like to be working continue to be excluded.[18]

What does this have to do with the benefits of an MLR? Had they been in common use five years ago, many now considered unemployable might still be in work, because the sort of MLR we are proposing is framed to find solutions for the issues that currently force many people out of work and/or make reemployment difficult.

The good news...

The impact of all of the government policies combined with the pressure on retirement incomes means that any employer willing to enable his older workers to remain in the workforce will often be pushing at an open door. When records began in 1992, workers aged fifty-plus accounted for 21% of UK employees: that figure is now 32%. This seismic shift means that 2.6% of adults aged between fifty and sixty-four are unemployed, the same rate as for people aged thirty-five to forty-nine.[19] Many have already moved beyond that point: according to figures released by

---

18 Business in the Community (2019) '1 Million More Older Workers By 2022: Update On Progress Towards Our Target'. www.bitc.org.uk/report/1-million-more-older-workers-by-2022-update-on-progress

19 Department for Work and Pensions Official Statistics (2019) 'Economic Labour Market Status of Individuals Aged 50 And Over, Trends Over Time'. www.gov.uk/government/statistics/economic-labour-market-status-of-individuals-aged-50-and-over-trends-over-time-september-2019

the Office for National Statistics in May 2019,[20] nearly one in nine men aged seventy and over are already working full or part-time: an increase of 137% over the past ten years. The number of women aged seventy and over still at work has more than doubled to 175,000.

Midlife Reviews: a brief history

In 2006, a group of careers professionals and labour market researchers published their thinking: that it would be advantageous for older workers to take a step back when they reach fifty or so, and review their options for the future – not just in the workplace, but also reflecting on how this exercise would cross over into other aspects of their life.[21] They made the point that individuals should not only understand their rights and opportunities, but also appreciate the potential financial risks of premature retirement.

The 'Ready for Ageing?' House of Lords report published early in 2013 gave further weight to the

---

20 Amelia Hill (2019) 'Number of Over-70s Still In Work More Than Doubles In A Decade', *The Guardian*. www.theguardian.com/money/2019/may/27/number-of-over-70s-still-in-work-more-than-doubles-in-a-decade

21 Stephen McNair (nd) 'A mid-life career review: making the older labour market work better for everyone', NIACE. https://www.assets.publishing.service.gov.uk/government/uploads/system/uploads/attachment_data/file/463892/mid-life-career-review-presentation.pdf

concept.[22] Its remit was to look at ways in which society could prepare for the challenges as well as maximise the opportunities of increasing longevity. Key to that was this recommendation: 'Employers should demonstrate more flexibility towards the employment of older workers, and help them to adapt, reskill and gradually move to more suitable roles and hours when they want to do so.' It also declared that 'cliff edge retirement should end', and that 'employers should support those with respon-sibilities for caring for older people – particularly people in their fifties or sixties who care for elderly parents – to continue part-time or in flexible work'.

While it doesn't mention the MLR as the means to enable this, it set the scene for it, as these actions are possible only by employer and employee moving towards a new way of discussing the future.

The next stage in the MLR's evolution was a major review undertaken between January 2013 and March 2015: The Department for Business, Innovation and Skills funded the National Institute for Adult Continuing Education, who worked with seventeen partner agencies to test a variety of models and pro-vide reviews to 2,883 clients.[23]

---

22 https://www.parliament.uk/business/committees/committees-a-z/lords-select/public-services-committee/report-ready-for-ageing/is-government-ready-for-ageing
23 Stephen McNair (nd) 'A Mid-Life Career Review: Making the older labour market work better for everyone', NIACE. https://assets.publishing.service.gov.uk/government/uploads/system/uploads/attachment_data/file/463892/mid-life-career-review-presentation.pdf

The reviews helped those who took part to better understand their career opportunities – whether that was to change jobs, become self-employed, negotiate more appropriate working conditions, or receive training to improve their employability. It also provided guidelines on how to make decisions about extending their working life and enhancing their health and wellbeing. These were low budget reviews (costing just £100 each) but even at that level, in the words of the final report, 'they helped people take stock of where they were and who they are, and what they wanted to achieve for the rest of their lives'. Their conclusion: 'The impact of the Review was considerable, participants had higher confidence and greater awareness of their options after their review... The project has provided the evidence to back the promotion of an MLR for all those who need one.'

With that evidence to call on, the concept was given a major boost by John Cridland's independent review of the SPA published in March 2017,[24] and engendered fears within government that the state pension was in danger of becoming unaffordable in the years to come. This review examined all the mechanisms needed to be in place if the SPA could realistically be advanced in the years ahead; among its recommendations was for individuals to take stock of all aspects of their

---

24 Department for Work and Pensions Independent report (2017) 'State Pension Age Independent Review: Final Report'. www.gov.uk/government/publications/state-pension-age-independent-review-final-report

lives – personal as well as professional. It concluded that, with 'often no natural trigger point which encourages people to do this,' life changing decisions were being made too late.

In John Cridland's words, 'As we live and work longer, many people now have more options and can make more choices. Yet there is relatively little help available in making those choices.' But there was, he concluded, an answer ready to hand: 'The Midlife MOT can act as a useful trigger to encourage people to take stock.'

But good ideas, even great ideas, often need more evidence and refining. The Centre for Ageing Better (the lottery-funded 'what works' body) then took the MLR to the next stage. Under their aegis, four pilot projects were independently undertaken in 2018 to test the design and value of an MLR covering three areas of focus: work, wealth and wellbeing. Aviva and Legal & General tried one approach: a series of face-to-face workshops; The Pensions Advisory Service another (a one-to-one pilot for self-employed workers), while Mercer developed and tested an online tool. This work is explored in detail in Chapter Ten as the different approaches taken highlight a range of potential methods of delivery.

The recent House of Lords Select Committee on Intergenerational Fairness and Provision (2019) 'Tackling Intergenerational Unfairness' report made the availability of a Midlife MOT one of their key recommendations – with several caveats.[25] They recognised that it 'would act as a trigger to encourage people to take stock, provide holistic advice to prepare for the transition and help workers to make realistic choices about work, health and retirement', saying that: 'We concur with Emma Stewart MBE, Chief Executive and Co-Founder of Timewise, who told us that midlife MOTs were "really about trying to instil the culture within an organisation that goes beyond any specific legislative requirement, in order to make sure those conversations can be had on a regular basis." Providing a single statutory MOT at a fixed age to every employee would lack flexibility and might lead to waste.'

The Committee also acknowledged the need for them to be conducted as part of a continuous responsibility of the employer, rather than a one-off event. Their key concern was that – to date – those providing the opportunity were larger employers with the resources to do that. This runs the risk that those working for smaller employers and the self-employed might miss out.

---

25 House of Lords Select Committee on Intergenerational Fairness and Provision: Report of Session 2017–19 'Tackling Intergenerational Unfairness'. www.publications.parliament.uk/pa/ld201719/ldselect/ldintfair/329/329.pdf

The Government's perspective

As part of our research towards this book, we asked the DWP about the role they see for the MLR going forwards. Here is what they had to say:

'In John Cridland's review of state pension age, he described how a Midlife MOT can act as a useful trigger to encourage people to take stock and described its value in helping older people return to employment, find appropriate training, make realistic decisions about extending their working lives and improve their health and finance, wellbeing at work and training and skills.

In 2018, the DWP worked with employers including the Civil Service, and other providers to research the level of user demand and potential scope of the MOT. Government believes that the Midlife MOT has the potential to act as a vital prompt to engage more people in planning more actively for later life. This is key to enabling the Department to meet its strategic objectives of ensuring financial security for current and future pensioners and supporting more people into work.

Throughout Summer 2018, Aviva, Legal and General and The Pensions Advisory Service carried out Midlife MOT pilots with their staff. The findings published by the Centre for Ageing Better, based on these pilots show that both employers and employees are convinced of the value of an MOT.

In February 2019, DWP launched an online web page which brings together work and skills, wellbeing, and financial elements of the Midlife MOT. To support employers, Business in The Community has also created MOT guides for employers.

Government is continuing to work with stakeholders to consider how best to signpost individuals to Midlife MOT information. The Government Business Champion for Older Workers, Andy Briggs, is sharing good practice and promoting the benefits of the MOT to other employers.'

PART ONE

THE EMPLOYEE PERSPECTIVE

ONE

Picture Your Future And Be 'Your Best You'

If you're somewhere north of forty-five and starting to wonder what life might hold in the years ahead, then this section is written specifically for you. Technically, you're middle-aged now. Hopefully that's a phrase you're comfortable with. It's often been regarded as a negative, but why should it be?

Research shows that your best years in terms of life satisfaction, happiness and even creativity may well be ahead of you, but to make sure you really do make the most of the years to come, being 'your best you' as positive psychologists would call it, you might want to start planning. Now. That's why the MLR can be a timely chance (or series of timely chances) to pause and reflect. An opportunity to inspect your finances, health and career, map out where you want to get to in the future and plan the best route to arrive there.

Ideally, this should be done (at least in part) in collaboration with your employer because they also have a vested interest in helping you achieve your objectives. Enabling you to be 'your best you' can also mean them employing your 'best you' too: someone in the right role, working to maximum effect.

An MLR is not like a regular annual work review, exploring how your job has been going for the last twelve months, whether you're due a raise and so on. The MLR is focused on the mid- to long-term and will look at your situation far more holistically: providing the starting point for reflection on your finances, work aspirations and overall wellbeing. It drills down to what your drivers are… personal as well as professional. It should be encouraging you to ask yourself some really important questions.

Like most processes, an MLR will only give you the right answers if you ask the right questions. So, to start the ball rolling, a question for you: where do you see yourself in five, ten, twenty, thirty years' time?

For instance:

- Do you see yourself as retired, do you want to still be working full-time, or would you like to start winding down towards retirement?

- Do you envisage yourself in another role, applying your life and work skills in a different way, perhaps running your own business or volunteering for causes you really care about?

- Would you like to be spending less time at work and more time on personal projects, or long-held ambitions?

- Do you want to see more of your family (for eg, play a major role in any grandchildren's lives)?

- Are you concerned about bettering your health and fitness?

- Do you have caring responsibilities that you're finding hard to combine with work?

- If you're looking to change career or start your own enterprise, do you have the skills in place to do that?

Now a second question: will you have the funds in place to be living the life you've just imagined? Indeed, do you even know how much you will have saved by the time you reach those benchmarks of ten, twenty or thirty years from now? Have you, or a financial adviser, ever calculated how much more you might need to save in the interim? Taking control of your future means taking control of your finances.

Finally, will your health be able to support you in that far-off imagined life or might you need to adjust your wellbeing and fitness regime to ensure it doesn't start to cause problems? It's not rocket science: the earlier you begin, the more chance you have of reaching your sixties, seventies, eighties and beyond in the physical shape to enjoy your later years.

Work, wealth and wellbeing are the three leg stools of most MLRs. The opportunity to look ahead and take control of your life. If you're a half-glass full sort of person, you're probably imagining all the positives achievable with more time for yourself and the things that matter to you. If you're a half-glass empty type, you may be worrying about whether you'll have enough money tucked away for a secure retirement, or what happens if poor health mars your later years. Either way, this book covers all the bases...

What does getting older mean to you?

For many, advancing age brings a gradual diminution of one's physical prowess, hopefully compensated for by an increasing understanding of oneself, one's work, others around you and the world. Our perspective evolves as some of the more fleeting pleasures lose their attraction and we recognise what provides us with real and lasting fulfilment.

According to research from the Centre for Economic Performance people report the highest levels of happiness between the age of fifty-five and eighty in their financial situation, their physical appearance and their overall wellbeing.[26] If you're currently finding life tough, you're not alone: the same research found that people reported the lowest levels of happiness between the ages of forty-five and fifty-nine.

Whether or not you make the most of your later years will depend on a number of factors. Not all are within your control, but many are – and that includes whether you are a positive or negative person. Why does that matter? According to scientists from the Boston University School of Medicine, people with greater optimism are actually more likely to live longer.[27] For the purposes of this book, we talked to two experts in their field to see how framing your future positively rather than negatively can make a huge difference to the outcome, and how, in that context, the MLR can provide the platform for a fulfilling life in the years leading up to and after work.

GUY ROBERTSON: RENOWNED RESEARCHER AND WRITER ON 'POSITIVE AGEING' AND 'AGEING WELL'

If you're looking to move towards a future where you age well, it makes sense to start thinking about it earlier than most people currently do. Waiting until you're on the cusp of retirement before you start thinking about what you're going to do in your life after work is not

26 Centre for Economic Performance Discussion paper (2019) 'A Happy Choice: Wellbeing as the Goal of Government'. http://cep.lse.ac.uk/pubs/download/dp1658.pdf

27 Gina DiGravio (2019) 'Optimists Live Longer', The Brink. www.bu.edu/articles/2019/optimists-live-longer

necessarily the end of the world. But if you want to start maximising your opportunities, it's better to start earlier.

Finance dominates most people's thinking about retirement, and many will not think much beyond that. But there's much more to reflect upon too. Most people are still locked into the narrative that you reach a certain age, stop work, start receiving a pension, then go off and have a nice life on the golf course.

However, there's ample evidence of the dangers of that kind of transition – especially if it's a sudden leap from full-time employment to never working again. That dramatic shift can be quite risky. We all need to prepare for later life, and key to that is having good connections with other people. Losing our work connections – as annoying as some of them might have been – can suddenly leave us at a loose end, and risking isolation and the poor mental health that goes along with that.

The MLR can also look at key aspects of a person's wellbeing and ensure they are prepared for the transition into retirement. 'Resilience' is the key to that, as life after work will come with new challenges. While some of us are born more resilient, resilience can be developed, and that is a central thesis of Cognitive Behavioural Therapy (CBT) and Positive Psychology: it's not what happens in life but how you interpret it. It's all about developing a mindset: thoughts are things you can change.

That's the context for looking, for instance, into how you might wind down from work rather than just stop suddenly. Given that people are living longer, do you want to work flat out until you're sixty-five, or whatever the magic number is, or would you rather reconsider your life, reduce the number of hours you work but carry on working for longer?

Allied to that is the whole issue of a sense of purpose – important to all of us, and one of the critical things in later life. Once you've done with the nine-to-five, what is going to get you out of bed in the morning? As part of MLR, I would always suggest envisioning what type of things you want to spend your time doing when you leave work. Pursuits such as painting and joining the National Trust are all very well, but if you want more than that out of life, you might think about the possibility of 'encore careers' where (on a paid or voluntary basis) you make more of the skills you've acquired over a lifetime.

Thinking about these possibilities sooner rather than later means you might consider what sort of training you may need to develop ahead of retirement.

From an employer's perspective, there's potentially a real win-win here too. Many companies are keen on corporate social responsibility initiatives, often getting their people to volunteer within the local community, but these are often low-skill tasks that, frankly, anyone could do. If employers could shift their focus towards developing their staff, they could help them build and apply skills within the workplace – such as mentoring – so they can later go on and work with young people.

Having a second bite at life

Tim Drake is the author of *Cherry Generation*. It eloquently sets out strategies for those planning to have a 'second bite of the cherry' in later life – focusing on what he describes as the 'four autonomies' of earning, learning, giving and recharging in order for an individual to 'be in control of who you are and what you do'. Now in his seventies, Tim describes himself as a 'promising youngster' – in his time he has founded and run businesses, think tanks and charities.

He is 'fascinated by unlocking potential', and to that end, his book encourages the reader to sit down and list the 'assets' they can bring to a future career or business. The experience and life skills you acquire and hone during a lifetime can be considerable: soft skills not always regarded highly but which are actually invaluable in many circumstances. Equally, he says, unlocking one's potential in later life is also about mindset – and the importance of regarding change as potentially positive rather than negative or challenging. The loss of prestige after leaving a career is a big thing for many. Their sense of self can be badly affected, but coping with this process, he maintains, is down to mindset. Managed and planned for correctly, the period of life after leaving a lifetime career can be hugely rewarding and satisfying.

TIM DRAKE: AUTHOR OF *CHERRY GENERATION*

A lot of *Cherry Generation* came out of a book I wrote called *You Can Be As Young As You Think*, which is about the difference between young brains and old brains. There's a lot of research across Europe around attitudes which shows that people start to 'age' at around eighteen and progress from there.

Most of our brains get older rather than remaining young – they become less flexible and adaptable to new circumstances and experiences. However, about 20% of people stay 'young brained' throughout their life. We've all met them: people who are just timeless. However, once you stop trying new things and taking on fresh challenges, you're finished.

Part of the difference is that old brains rely on planning ahead. They read the instructions and follow them. When things go wrong, that can be a setback from which some people never recover. Young brains say: 'I know my goal. I'll duck and dive all the way until I get there.' They just do it on the hoof. 'I may not actually be where I want to be at the moment, but while I'm here I'll adjust to my circumstances...' So older brains, if they want to renew their lives rather than simply keep doing the same old same old, need to think more like younger brains and – while having a long-term goal – be prepared to adjust to changing situations and the inevitable unexpected fork in the road.

Young people will define themselves differently too, because they are quite happy to be described as 'slashees' – earning money in a number of different ways, rather than just one. Portfolio careers are the same. They show a willingness to not be bound by what they started out as and reflect all the different things they can successfully take on in life. If older people can adopt that 'young brain' thinking, they will be better equipped for life after their first career ends.

Mentoring is one new role that older people can take on and builds on their knowledge and experience of relationships. Where it's done right, it's brilliant. I provided mentoring within prisons for twenty-five years and also did some training with Samaritans; and I discovered that what you couldn't ever give was any advice – whatsoever. Listen and listen, until the right thing to do becomes their idea. It's how consultants operate too.

Finally, one of the words that appears throughout my book is 'fulfilment', and there's a reason for that. Purpose is the modern thing: 'I need a purpose', and 'everybody needs a purpose'.

I never knew what I wanted to do when I left school. I still don't. I don't feel I particularly have a 'purpose'. However, I want to do things that I find fulfilling. They can be all over the place – completely random – without any golden thread linking them all.

Fulfilling roles can be voluntary – and so can being a grandparent. If you're thinking about the future, and recognise that you're not going to be in this high-performing job for the next forty years, stop and think: what could that fulfilling future look like?

TWO

Manage Your Money, Manage Your Life

Money isn't everything, and it can't buy you happiness (although it has been known to relieve some of the misery) but planning ahead really begins with our finances.

Agreed, most of us, when asked, put relationships at the top of our list of life priorities. Our careers can really matter to us too, or perhaps the voluntary work we'd like to do if only we had more time and greater financial freedom, but if we don't enjoy the luxury of good health, it's harder to do many of the things that perhaps we'd like. 'Wealth' is the first topic we deal with in detail in this book because having control of your financial situation is pivotal if you are going to maximise the MLR process.

Knowledge, as ever, is key to having control. Knowing how much we need to live on in the years ahead, and comparing that with how much we are currently accumulating, is the crucial first step we must make with the MLR – critical in determining:

- How long we need to keep on earning
- When (or if) we could ever afford to move sideways or downwards from our current job if that's what we'd really like to do
- Whether we could afford to wind down and do fewer hours
- Whether we could take a sabbatical or time out to assume care responsibilities etc

Large numbers of us don't have that financial information to hand. Indeed, according to recent research from Aviva,[28] almost nine million midlife employees are currently 'flying blind into retirement', oblivious to how much pension they will receive, or even whether it will be enough to secure a comfortable retirement. Further, a worrying two out of five employees do not even have a handle on how much their state pension will be worth – despite the fact that this will represent a large proportion of many people's retirement income.

---

28 AVIVA Research (2019) 'Nine Million UK Mid-Life Employees Flying Blind Into Retirement'. www.aviva.com/newsroom/news-releases/2019/08/nine-million-uk-mid-life-employees-flying-blind-into-retirement

While you might think that it's younger people who are less likely to have a fix on their future incomes, many in older age brackets are still hiding their heads in the sand, not least because the pensions landscape has altered radically in recent years.

In the same research study, the newly introduced pension freedom (intended in part to encourage people to take more control of their retirement finances) has added to the confusion: some 62% of employees aged over forty-five are unaware of what their options are, while 37% do not even know what type of pension scheme they are in.

Why is this so important? In the cautionary words of Lindsey Rix, Managing Director of savings and retirement at Aviva: 'Without a clear picture of what they currently have saved or might need to save for a comfortable retirement, many UK employees are approaching retirement with their eyes closed – with no realistic idea of how near or far they are from their destination.'

Does that sound like you? Flying blind, with no clear picture of your finances? Or have you got it all sewn up? If you really think there's nothing you need to know, feel free to skip this section, but even if you're a pensions and savings whizz, it might just provide a few useful tips...

Why the MLR can be a great wake-up call

Whatever stage you're at in your life, knowing where you stand with your finances can provide you with the stimulus to take action before it's too late and allow you to sleep easy at night knowing you've got all the bases covered. The MLR can provide a great opportunity to do just that.

Another recent piece of research by Aegon, published in their 'Retirement Confidence Survey' revealed that a fraction over half of UK workers (52%) say they are confident about their ability to retire comfortably – a slight increase on 2017 when it was 48%.[29]

The survey also found that:

- 10% of us don't have any pension savings

- 25% of those with pension savings don't know how much they hold in pensions

- 36% have never estimated their income needs for retirement

Here is another disturbing statistic: a 2019 report issued by the World Economic Forum, which looked

---

29 Aegon (2019) 'Retirement Confidence is On The Rise But Overconfidence Carries Risks'. www.cofunds.aegon.co.uk/ukcpw/intermediary/ news/retirement_confidenceisontherisebutoverconfidencecarriesrisks. html

globally at the future of pensions, says that pension savings in the UK are on average likely to run out 10.3 years before death, with women running out even earlier, at 12.6 years.[30] The cause, they say, is increasing longevity which has not been matched by increases in savings for pensions.

Your income in retirement

So, how much income can we expect to look forward to after we leave work? If we aren't to continue working in some capacity, the first step is to determine how much we currently have saved in the form of pensions, savings and assets, and what that might generate as a pension income.

Your state pension

Getting all your 'ducks in a row' with your state pension entitlements (and any required National Insurance contributions) is a really important first step in your MLR. The UK state pension could never be described as generous. In fact, according to data from the Organisation for Economic Co-operation and Development (OECD),[31] the UK state pension

---

30 Tom Bailey (2019) 'British Pensioners Are Running Out of Money A Decade Too Early', Moneywise. www.moneywise.co.uk/news/2019-06-17%E2%80%8C%E2%80%8C/british-pensioners-are-running-out-money-decade-too-early

31 OECD 'Pensions At A Glance 2019'. www.oecd.org/publications/oecd-pensions-at-a-glance-19991363.htm

is the worst in the developed world. Expressed as a percentage of average earnings, UK retirees receive a meagre 29% of the average wage through the state pension. That's just behind Mexico in a list topped by the Netherlands (100.6%), followed by Portugal (94%) and Italy (93.2%). The average across the OECD is 62.9%. Thankfully, many of us will be more reliant on a private or company pension for our retirement income – but don't ignore your state pension. Despite it being so low, it can still form an important part of your retirement income.

So how much will yours be? The full new state pension (from April 2020) is £175.20 per week – £9,110.40 a year. That helpfully goes up annually in line with the 'Triple Lock' guarantee by the Government made in 2010: a pledge to increase the state pension every year by the higher rate – of inflation, average earnings or a minimum of 2.5%. (As this book goes to press that guarantee still applies, but it has been a source of political contention for some time.)

However, to receive the full state pension, caveats do apply. You only qualify to receive it when you reach a given age. This is currently rising in stages towards sixty-six by October 2020, reaching sixty-seven between 2026 and 2028 and onto sixty-eight at some point between 2037 and 2039. This timetable is also under review (and some political pressure), so when you do make plans for the future, check when you

are likely to receive yours by going to www.gov.uk/
state-pension-age.

Receiving the state pension also relies on how much
you have paid in over the years. You'll need at least
ten qualifying years on your National Insurance (NI)
record – although they do not have to be ten succes-
sive years. If you weren't in full-time employment,
you may also qualify for some of those years through
National Insurance credits – for example, if you were
unemployed; ill or a parent or carer; made voluntary
contributions; or paid married women's or widow's
reduced rate contributions. To receive the full amount,
you will need thirty-five qualifying years of NI contributions, and for every year you haven't made an NI
contribution, you lose 1/35th of your entitlement.

There are ways to boost that amount: you can opt to
defer it if you think you can get by, and this will help
increase its value as well as reduce your income tax
liability during that period. You can defer it as long as
you wish, and every year you do so will increase future
payments by some 5.8%. Also worth noting is the fact
that once you have reached SPA you no longer need
to make NI contributions – even if you are working
full-time. Deciding when you receive your state pension can play an important part in your MLR planning,
especially if you are considering working past the SPA.

So how much will you receive? This can be easily
determined by contacting the Future Pension Centre:

www.gov.uk/future-pension-centre (tel: 0800 731 0175). As well as telling you how many NI contributions you have made to date, they can also give advice on making additional voluntary contributions to make up for lost years. Looked at in comparison with other pension savings, the state pension is actually quite a sound place to 'invest' in this way, but there are time limits on catching up from previous years. Royal London have produced a handy guide detailing all of your options.[32]

Finally, there is a safety net if you aren't entitled to a full new state pension and you have no other income – Pension Credit. For more on that, go to www.gov.uk/pension-credit.

Private pensions

While state pensions are a good base for a retirement income, they won't provide more than that – a rather meagre 'base' or safety net. A recent *Which?* Report which drew on thousands of retired *Which?* members to see where their money was being spent, found that couples on around £27,000 a year (£20,000 for individuals living on their own) could cover all the basic areas of expenditure together with a few extras, such

---

32 Royal London (2018) 'Topping Up Your State Pension: Everything you ever wanted to know 2018/2019'. www.royallondon.com/siteassets/site-docs/media-centre/good-with-your-money-guides/topping-up-your-state-pension-guide.pdf

as holidays, hobbies and eating out.[33] This went up to £42,000 a year (£33,000 for an individual) if they wanted to enjoy luxuries such as long-haul holidays and a new car every five years.

Those figures are well beyond the scope of the state pension, so private pensions to the rescue, then? Well, yes, or possibly no – because that will depend on what you've managed to tuck away during your lifetime. To understand how your pension can fund your future, let's look at how most of us accrue a retirement income.

The most popular are defined contribution (DC) pensions where we build up a pot of money (or a number of pots if we have changed jobs) over the years, and which have usually been invested into a mix of shares, bonds and property. That builds in value over the years (helped by tax relief from the Government and contributions from our employer) depending upon the performance of the investments.

Remember that you can access the money in a private pension pot earlier than the state pension: while this will depend on your pension scheme's rules, it's usually after you're fifty-five, although you may be able to take money out before this age if you're retiring early because of ill health. At the point of accessing your

---

33 Which? Money (2019) 'How Much Will You Need To Retire?' www.which.co.uk/money/pensions-and-retirement/starting-to-plan-your-retirement/how-much-will-you-need-to-retire-atu0z9k0lw3p

pot you can also elect to withdraw a tax-free lump of cash (typically 25%) and move the rest into either a drawdown pension or an annuity.

This can have implications for your MLR: in terms of boosting your income should you elect to retire early or wind down at work, fifty-five is an age when you can start factoring in pension income. Obviously there is a 'wealth warning' attached to this: the earlier you do access your pension pot (or pots), the more it will impact upon your future income, so you really do need to have done your sums if you go down this route.

Taking money out at this stage could be a useful way of starting a business or investing in something other than a pension (shares or a property, for instance) but it has consequences for your retirement income and needs thinking through carefully – ideally guided by professional advice. The longer you leave your pension pot intact and growing, the more you should be able to draw from it in each subsequent year.

Pension drawdown vs an annuity

In the past, the conventional route was to invest in an annuity: effectively turning a lump sum into a regular amount guaranteed either for a fixed term or for life, but the introduction of pension freedoms under George Osborne has radically changed the landscape by giving savers far more flexibility with what they do with their pension pot(s).[34] Once you reach the age of fifty-five, you will be in a position to take the money contained in your pension pot(s) and use it to generate an income.

The difference between an annuity and a pension drawdown is that an annuity is a type of retirement income product that you buy with some or all of your pension pot. It pays a guaranteed regular retirement income either for life or for a set period. Pension drawdown is a way of using your pension pot to provide you with a regular retirement income, but the income you get will vary depending on the pension fund's performance. It isn't guaranteed for life. The advantage of an annuity has always been security. It has also traditionally allowed a modicum of flexibility in the form of providing an income for a partner or building in annual increases to allow for inflation. Those who have certain potentially life-limiting conditions, or smoke, can also purchase an enhanced version, which pays out slightly more generously, while a variable annuity allows someone to benefit if the investments in the fund perform better than expected.

The big disadvantage for many thinking about an annuity (particularly in recent years) has been their relatively poor performance. According to recent research from Moneyfacts.co.uk, income payable from the average annuity has fallen steeply: an average single life standard annual annuity income for someone at

---

34 HM Revenue & Customs News Story (2015) 'Pension Changes 2015'. www.gov.uk/government/news/pension-changes-2015

sixty-five now stands at just £4,100 for every £100,000 invested, while an average enhanced annuity income will yield £4,750.[35] Compare this to the golden years of annuities such as 1995, when a sixty-five year old man buying a standard 'level' annuity with a £100,000 pension pot would have typically received an annual pay-out of £11,100. The drop in returns reflects poor performance in ultra-safe investments such as bonds, together with increasing life expectancies.

If you opt for a drawdown pension, it's important to know how much you can safely withdraw from it. If you've had a generous employer and you've been fortunate or savvy enough to tuck away a tidy pension pot, you could be looking forward to a comfortable retirement. Here is a rather alarming statistic that should give many people in Britain reason to worry about their future though: according to the Financial Conduct Authority, the average amount that people have in their DC pension pot when they retire is just £61,897 (and that figure masks the fact that 40% of pension pots have less than £10,000 in them).[36] If you took out what is widely regarded as a safe level of income – 4% – that would give you the princely sum of around £2,500 a year. Even more alarming is the statistic that the average drawdown of pensions is

---

35 Derin Clark (2019) 'Annuity Incomes Fall to Historic Low'. www.moneyfacts.co.uk/news/retirement/annuity-incomes-fall-to-historic-low

36 Patrick Collinson (2019) 'Five Figures That Show Why You Should Be Worried About Pensions', *The Guardian*. www.theguardian.com/money/2019/sep/28/uk-pensions-saving-retirement

much higher than that: 8% to be precise, which would soon leave the retiree without a proverbial pot…

If your aspirations are somewhat higher than that, a £1,055,000 pension pot (the current lifetime allowance before you start paying 55% tax) would give you a tad over £40,000 a year with a (relatively conservative) return of 4%. Of course, most of us who have pension pots building up will be somewhere in between those two figures.

Taking out your pension pot as cash

You are also allowed to take out your pension pot in the form of cash and place it in a deposit or savings account. Any future amount you take out is tax-free for the first 25%. Unless you have other reliable sources of income, this route does carry the risk of paying more tax than you might otherwise do, and of running out in the future. If you have a particularly large pension pot, one option is to take out up to 25% tax-free and then invest that in a buy-to-let property. Going down that road requires expert advice – more on that shortly.

Defined benefit (final salary or career average) pensions

Defined Benefit (DB) pensions are widely regarded as the 'gold standard' of pensions as the provider (normally a large employer or the public sector) guarantees you a certain amount each year when you retire based on a combination of your salary, the number of years you served and a multiplier calculation made under the rules of your pension scheme.

You and your employer can contribute to the scheme and they will be responsible for ensuring there will be enough money to pay your pension income. They will often continue to pay a pension to your spouse, civil partner or dependents when you die, and quite possibly a lump sum too. While most DB schemes have a retirement age of sixty-five, you may well be able to access it from fifty-five onwards but this will affect how much you can expect to receive. You should also be able to defer your pension until past sixty-five if you wish.

You can also take out 25% of the whole pension from the age of fifty-five as a tax-free lump sum, or earlier if you are seriously ill, if the pension is worth less than £10,000, or if the total value of all your pension savings is less than £30,000.

Transferring your defined benefit pension

The introduction of pensions freedom in 2015 means that from fifty-five you now have the option to transfer your private sector DB pension or funded public sector scheme to a DC pension – as long as you do so before you begin receiving payments. This has received a lot of press coverage over concerns that savers are moving away from what is seen as a 'gold plated' pension. The attraction is that some employers are incentivising pension scheme members to transfer, and the transfer values of DB schemes have risen significantly in recent times. There have also been a large number of scams reported where DB pension members have been cold-called and tempted to transfer to make an investment in a scheme apparently offering exceptionally high returns. The advice is always the same: if a scheme sounds too good to be true, the reason is usually because it is. If someone is calling you out of the blue with an offer you seemingly can't refuse, they are almost certainly not from a reputable provider.

It is always a good idea to take expert advice from a regulated financial adviser before you make any decision – and this is obligatory if your pension savings are worth £30,000 or more. As attractive as the alternative may appear, you will be giving up some valuable benefits which may not apply with an alternative scheme. If you're currently in an unfunded DB pension scheme (such as teachers and other public sector schemes), you will not be able to transfer your pension pot to a DC pension scheme, although you will still be able to transfer to another DB pension scheme.

Other sources of income

On top of your pension fund, you may have decided to tuck money away into a savings account such as an Individual Savings Account (ISA). This is a helpful way to tuck money away for your retirement, especially if you are in danger of exceeding your £40,000 annual pension contribution cap or you are heading to exceed the £1,055,000 lifetime allowance.

For purposes of an income in later life, this will typically be a Lifetime ISA. You are currently allowed to put in up to £4,000 each year until you reach the age of fifty. The Government will add a 25% bonus to your savings up to a maximum of £1,000 per year. The Lifetime ISA limit of £4,000 counts towards your annual ISA limit (currently £20,000). You can also put money each year into other forms of ISA – cash, stocks and shares or innovative finance. You can hold either cash or stocks and shares in your Lifetime ISA or have a combination of both.

When you turn fifty you will not be able to place any further money in your Lifetime ISA or earn the 25% bonus but your account will stay open and your savings will still earn interest or investment returns. You can only begin to withdraw money from your Lifetime ISA when you reach the age of sixty or if you become terminally ill with less than twelve months to live or you'll pay a 25% charge.

Property investments

One in ten UK adults own a second home,[37] some 5.5 million people, with half of the properties owned by baby boomers (born between 1946 and 1965) and a quarter owned by the succeeding Generation X. Many of these will be purchased as a buy-to-let investment, and while that class of asset has had much of its shine knocked off it following policy and tax changes over recent years, for those who are already buy-to-let landlords, rental income can form an important part of their retirement plans.

While this is a solid 'bricks and mortar' investment which on past performance is likely (but not certainly) to increase in value over the years, it is not immune to negative factors such as:

- Occupational voids which can knock a hole in returns

- Ongoing need for repairs and refurbishments – especially with older properties and HMOs (house in multiple occupation)

- The cost of safety checks, maintenance, insurance, advertising and agents' fees

---

37 Resolution Foundation (2019) 'Additional property wealth across Britain is up more than 50 per cent this century to almost £1 trillion'. www.resolutionfoundation.org/press-releases/additional-property-wealth-across-britain-is-up-more-than-50-per-cent-this-century-to-almost-1-trillion

- Being an 'illiquid' asset – that is, it could take a long time to realise its full value if you ever wish to cash it in

- The associated costs of selling

If you are considering reinvesting savings and assets into a buy-to-let property and using that as a retirement income, it's well worth doing a great deal of research first. The better yields are likely to come (perhaps not surprisingly) on older properties in less fashionable areas – often acting as HMOs for students or others on low incomes.[38]

While the yields are often tempting, they come with caveats in terms of additional costs of managing and maintaining the property (unless you plan to do much of the work yourself). You can offset some of the costs against tax and even take out a buy-to-let mortgage to help fund a larger investment if you think the sums add up, but you will pay over the odds when purchasing the property in the form of 3% additional stamp duty: a property north of £250,000 will attract stamp duty of at least 8%, something which will definitely knock a hole in your initial returns.

Other investments

These can range from stock market portfolios through to premium bonds, antiques and classic cars – some

---

38 'UK Buy-to-Let Yield Map 2019/2020'. www.totallymoney.com/buy-to-let-yield-map

of which will be more 'liquid' than others. Premium bonds will see your money reduce in real value year on year unless you notch up a win or two, while any asset that can fluctuate in value according to taste comes with a wealth warning and is best regarded as a hobby where you can afford to lose some of your outlay. Savings accounts will, in the main, offer a higher rate of interest the longer you are prepared to lock your money into them, but typically these will be relatively low rates of return compared to many other forms of investments.

Inheriting money in the future

In the process of assessing your future sources of income, there may be the prospect of an inheritance. Unless this is a guaranteed amount at a fixed point in time, make sure that any plans you make take account of the fact that an elderly relative may live far longer than you anticipate, or may need expensive care for an extended period.

Have you mislaid a pension along the way?

The Association of British Insurers recently estimated that more than 1.6 million pension pots worth £19.4bn are currently 'lost' – the equivalent of £13,000 per plan.[39] Many of us have moved jobs over the years, forgetting that we've squirreled away contributions towards a company pension or assuming that there is nothing to claim as the company has been taken over or ceased trading. Could that be you?

Finding out really isn't that tricky and doesn't cost anything apart from a modicum of effort and perhaps some postage. Most pension schemes are obliged to send you a statement each year. This will include an estimate of the retirement income that the pension pot might generate when you reach a given age, but people move homes and forget to pass on their new information. If you know which pension provider your pension was with, contact them with the information they need: your plan number, date of birth, NI number and (if you have it) the date when your pension was set up. To trace a workplace pension run by an employer, get in touch with them, giving your NI number and the dates when you joined and left them. Alternatively, as a 'catch all', you can contact the Pension Tracing Service (0845 6002 537 or www.findpensioncontacts.service.gov.uk). This is a free service containing a database of more than 200,000 workplace and personal pension schemes. They'll be able to give you the contact details of whoever is now managing the pension fund you think you may have contributed to who, in turn, will need your NI

---

39 Harvey Jones (2019) 'The Lost £19bn: How to trace those forgotten pension pots' *The Observer*. www.theguardian.com/money/2019/may/12/lost-pension-funds-pots-auto-enrol-track-trace

number and times of joining and leaving the scheme or place of work. This can be particularly helpful if your old employer has merged or gone out of business or if the pension provider has been taken over by another company – pension schemes usually survive these situations as they are managed separately.

One good reason to check up on a pension pot like this is that some schemes aren't well managed, and fees can often erode returns. Transferring them or consolidating your pension pots could prove a sensible move long-term – again, expert advice is always advisable. Finally, beware of scammers who offer to find your pension pot for you – no one should ask for money to do this.

Hunting down other lost assets and savings

If you have any old savings accounts or investments and haven't heard from the providers for some time, it might be a matter of them not knowing your current address. Either contact the provider direct or try the Unclaimed Assets Register (www.uar.co.uk) – a service run by Experian which will charge you a small fee for helping you reclaim your money. www.mylostaccount.org.uk is an equivalent, free service which allows you to you search for accounts with thirty banks, forty-three building societies and National Savings and Investments (NS&I).

Transferring your DC pension(s)

You have the option to transfer some or all of your DC pots to a different provider and this can be an attractive option if your current provider is not performing well, charges relatively high fees or doesn't offer some of the benefits you are looking for. If you are moving to another country, you might also want to transfer it to a provider there. Taking professional expert advice can be really important before you make this decision.

Thinking of combining your pension pots?

The same advice – speak to an expert – applies if you are one of the many people who have worked for more than one employer and have more than one DC pension pot. Combining them will make them easier to manage and possibly help you save on fees but keeping all of these pots separate will enable you to 'spread your bets' somewhat as each will perform differently over the years. It will also allow you the option to take one earlier to tide you over while the other(s) continue growing.

Now add all your assets and potential income streams up

That's a run through of some of the main types of savings you may have built up for your retirement. Other assets can apply, but will it all be enough to fund the retirement you've planned for yourself? Getting to grips with your assets and future potential income is the first stage in the MLR process. The next one is understanding your options going forwards – in particular, knowing how to best manage your resources and whether or not you need to make any changes to live the life you want to in the years ahead. On to the next chapter.

THREE

Financial Planning

Will your income in retirement be enough?

Armed with the information we've just run through you should now be in a better position to start assessing what sort of income you are likely to be able to enjoy when you stop work. This will allow you to make an informed decision on when you can retire, wind down or change roles, but unless you have the tools to precisely assess what your income and outgoings are likely to be, it will be difficult to arrive at more than an educated guess.

Spending even a little time at this point with a financial adviser can prove beneficial as they can look at your savings and pensions in the round. Using specialist software, they will crunch the numbers and tell you what each of your investments and pensions is likely to yield at any given point in the future, as well as advise you on what your options are in terms of moving them about, saving more, or taking steps to reduce your outgoings. They will also be able to advise you which of your various income streams to tap into should you look to part-retire in the future – the ones that maximise your future income and minimise any tax liabilities.

Even if you walk away from a meeting having learned nothing new, the peace of mind that comes with knowing you're doing the right thing can prove invaluable. It's just as likely, though, that you'll come away with a fresh perspective on how to maximise your chances of a comfortable retirement. An adviser will have many insights that a layman will not, no matter how good you are with your finances.

Weaving this into your MLR thinking

The first, basic step is to calculate what sort of income you need to sustain the lifestyle you want after you stop working. This can be tricky, as you might not know precisely what you'll need in the future, and it's impossible to predict the exact impact of inflation, but an adviser will be able to outline the broad scenarios.

They can also see whether your current plans for saving and work put you on a trajectory to receive that income when you need it, or whether you need to save more. Some employees find they've been rooted to the same contribution rates since they started work – perhaps as little as 5%. If you can afford to do so, maximise your pension pot. A conversation with an adviser can help you revisit your pension portfolio and determine whether the balance between risk vs returns is still the one you want, or whether you need to move it. As you get closer to the point when you want to receive your money, it makes general sense to dial down the risk. When you're younger, you've got more time for returns to bounce back after a difficult period. Your attitude towards other factors may also have changed since you first set out – for instance, you might feel strongly that you now want to focus on ethical investments.

You should also take a look at insurance policies which might have a bearing on your decisions in this area, as well as the situation with your pension(s).

Why not dig a little deeper?

The MLR can also be an excellent opportunity to look at all your finances and include other aspects of your outgoings, liabilities and income: a platform for making sure you maximise every penny coming into your account in the vital years ahead.

For instance:

- Should you try to clear your debts, especially if they are relatively expensive ones?

- Would it be better to extend your mortgage, allowing for the fact that you intend to work longer, or perhaps borrow more on your mortgage to clear expensive debts?

- Should you try to clear your mortgage to reduce your liabilities in the years ahead, or would the money be put to better use on other things, such as increasing your pension contributions or taking out a life insurance policy?

- Are there ways to reduce your outgoings – such as memberships you rarely use, or switching utility suppliers?

- Are you making the best use of your credit cards, or are you paying interest unnecessarily?

- Could you transfer your credit card debt or overdraft onto another card offering interest-free credit for a year or more?

- If you have a small surplus available, is it worth tucking it away? Sometimes expensive surprises come along, such as replacing a broken boiler or booking an emergency flight, and it pays to be ready with a go-to fund rather than taking on expensive short-term debt.

- Have you got adequate policies in place to protect your family should you die, fall ill or have to give up work? If you are heading towards an unsustainable future, is it worth considering downsizing to reduce your overheads and allow you to pump more into your pension?

- Are there household economies you might start sooner rather than wait until you retire?

Reducing or clearing credit card debt can be a really effective way to reduce your outgoings: £1,000 of unpaid credit card debt, for instance, could easily lead to about £250 in interest over the course of twelve months. Not only do you need to consider the hard numbers, you also need to factor in the detrimental effect unpaid credit card debt might have on your credit rating. The higher your rating, the cheaper it is to borrow. There are a number of reputable online agencies which will tell you how you are viewed by lenders. Check out your options before signing up – a basic service should be free. Identify the negatives against your name, challenge them if they are inaccurate, then take steps to improve your rating.

Maximising your future income

Based on the conversation you have with an adviser, you can then consider whether you would be better off putting more money into your pension pot or using it elsewhere (for instance, clearing any borrowing or overpaying your mortgage).

Remember, the UK Government will effectively boost your contributions to your pension pot in the form of tax relief. Basic rate taxpayers get 20% tax relief on their contributions, and higher rate taxpayers receive 40% (subject to contribution limits). Effectively, that means that it 'costs' basic rate taxpayers £80 to put £100 towards their pension. For those in the higher rate it would 'cost' £60. That's quite a saving – and bear in mind that (as of the tax year 2019-20) you'll get tax relief on pension contributions of up to 100% of your earnings or a £40,000 annual allowance, whichever is lower. You can also carry forward unused allowances from the last three years on the condition that you were a member of a pension scheme during those years.

FOUR

Health And Wellbeing

So, onto the second 'leg' of the MLR stool: your health and wellbeing.

No MLR is complete unless a individuals take the opportunity to reflect upon how well their minds and bodies are standing up to the rigours of life – and whether they will need to make any changes if they are to fulfil their financial and career ambitions.

Someone who has made her mark advising on how to go about this process is health coach, Joanna Shurety. She works on behalf of businesses to improve the physical and mental health of their workforce as well as many individual professionals. The reason that some enlightened companies are prepared to pay for her services is quite simple: a healthy employee is a more productive one.

JOANNA SHURETY, SHURETY COACHING, HEALTH COACH

For companies keen to maximise their most important asset, it's the next logical step from hiring business coaches to improve the skills, motivation and focus of their personnel. Your talent, your productivity and your professional excellence are completely reliant on a healthy body and mind. Without good health, your performance will be severely compromised.

And if it makes sense for an employer to help their staff to be healthier, it certainly makes sense for the employee too – and 'midlife' (when signs of 'wear and tear' may have already started to show) is a significant point in your life to really focus on the small but important changes that could not only make you feel far better in the short-term, but give you many more years of healthy living. Living longer but having a poor quality of life due to ill health is not a prospect many consider.

Most of us will reach our forties and fifties after years on the proverbial treadmill, busting a gut to make our way up the career ladder, get the bills paid and possibly raising a family along the way. Pausing to check whether or not this is actually doing us harm is essential if we aren't to run the real risk of getting to our 60s unable to work or to fully enjoy our lives.

We continually push onwards, convinced that if we work hard enough and long enough, we'll get promoted or paid more. The reality is that for many, the punishing workload and those long hours take a toll well before we ever reach the destination, with costly work absences from stress and burn-out ever on the increase. It's not that we don't know that how we live affects our health, we just don't have the time, energy or support to do the stuff we know we should be doing to keep healthy.

Look on it as a dripping tap. We can all build up bad habits over a period of time, around our sleep, not relaxing, exercise, drinking too much than is good for us, etc. When you're younger, if you have a bad week, you can generally recover from that. But if you're doing that stuff over years it eventually catches up with you.

The good news is that it is never too late to change our habits. We all have a choice to do something differently (be it big or small), and bit by bit we can turn our health around. The challenge is finding habits that work for us as individuals and that we will stick to. Indefinitely.

There's tons of information out there on what constitutes a healthy lifestyle. Most people know what they should be doing. They just haven't found ways to adopt and sustain it. If you have not tackled the 'why' you do certain things, your mindset, relationship with yourself, body and food then change is difficult to make stick. The key is to make gradual changes to upgrade lifestyle choices. It is what you do on a daily basis that really counts, creates a habit and makes a difference to your health.

If you feel tired and lethargic, you're not at your best, you're just existing. What you eat and drink, how you think, what you do and if you move or exercise your body are all connected and will impact on your health long-term. Fitness and wellness should be at the centre of every person's work/life balance. If you feel more energised you feel more confident, more engaged, more creative, more able to deal with the pressures and crises that crop up, more willing to get involved.

Start making the changes

So, as part of their MLR, what can people in their forties and fifties do to improve their health and well-being and so extend their potential for continuing to work into later life if that is what they want to do?

It's looking at small changes that you can add to your routine that will make a huge impact on your resilience and energy – the balance of food, hydration, sleep, relaxation, putting yourself a little bit further up the agenda – but without having to spend a lot of time, money or effort. If you perceive this as an effort, you could well fall at the first hurdle. Start by looking honestly at how you feel and ask yourself: do I really want to feel like this (or perhaps even worse) for the next twenty years?

Going for a health check – through your employer or privately to your doctor or pharmacy – is often a great start as it will give you a 'benchmark' to progress from. Having your heart rate, blood pressure, weight and cholesterol level measured, acknowledging how much alcohol you consume or whether you smoke, being honest about how much exercise you are regularly getting, whether you're sleeping well, feeling energetic or lethargic, motivated or depressed are all important factors to consider. Reflecting and recognising that we need to move on from where we are is usually straightforward. For some, it's improving their sleep, for others it's reducing the stress in their lives or improving their nutrition.

For many in stressful jobs, their coping mechanism is alcohol. While that may work for a few hours, it disrupts sleep so the next day starts badly and these individuals feel dehydrated and fatigued. Hydration is a massive one for many of us working in offices, especially in those with air-conditioning. Often stuck at our desks without moving for hours at a time, we're also not getting out enough for the fresh air our bodies need. Our bodies need to keep moving – that doesn't necessarily mean going to the gym every day, it can be as simple as walking for ten minutes.

Monitoring progress can be a big motivation for some as they can really see what they need to change – and measure their response by results, so Fitbits, apps such as MapMyRun or Strava, targets in the gym for a 2k row or just keeping a diary of changes in your weight, body fat, pulse and blood pressure can all help. A lot of people like that sort of evidence base. Heart monitors can also be good in some instances, for eg, they can indicate when those under stress need to relax.

Bear in mind that what works for someone else isn't necessarily going to be the right thing for you when it comes to exercise. Taking up running can be a great way to get fit, and the 'Couch to 5k' challenge is an excellent incentive to kick off, but if you're overweight the pounding on your knees when you start is likely to be more harmful than helpful and may actually put you out of action. Far better to shed some pounds first by cycling or using a step or rowing machine in the gym. Swimming is far better for older joints and exercises more muscles. Importantly, do something you enjoy, and which can fit in with the rest of your life. Most importantly: start slowly if you don't want to end quickly. The road to being well is paved with good intentions.

Why our mental health is something to think about too

While most of us can see quick fixes to improve our physical wellbeing, making changes that will help our mental wellbeing can sometimes prove more problematic. By exercising more, getting better hydration, more sleep and better nutrition, together with limiting your alcohol intake, you're investing in your body, doing things that make it physically stronger. Your body operates better, and you are preventing a physical decline in your health. The same applies mentally.

A lot of people have forgotten how to relax. They've lost the art of just switching off, believing they have to fill every moment and ending up feeling bombarded. While it's not necessarily a bad thing in itself, there's not a start and end time for social media – it's 24/7. They might be reading, going for a walk or chatting to their family but checking their phones at the same time.

How does this fit into an MLR?

However, while our personal lives can be sources of stress, so too can our jobs. Some companies expect a huge amount from their employees and some people can simply take more pressure than others. If you're finding the strain of work is too much for you, make changes to your life that you can control and which will reduce the pressure: make sure your body is as healthy as it can be, make time to really relax when you can. You really can improve your natural 'resilience' or 'bounce back-ability'.

If that's not working, you have to be open about your limits. How the company responds to that will tell you an awful lot about them. It can help you decide whether working for them long-term is right for you or not. What can come out of these conversations is a recognition that a more flexible approach is needed: you may need to step back from the role you are doing, do fewer hours, or perhaps work from home once a week. Critically, if you've made yourself the 'best you can be' by reflecting upon your wellbeing and making the positive changes that you feel able to make, you will be in the best position to navigate the rest of your career.

Getting into shape

If you have concerns about your physical wellbeing, even small ones, then this section is for you as we draw the rule over what constitutes being 'healthy' and what could be described as 'could do better'. It also allows you to set yourself some targets if that will help you achieve your objectives.

Your weight

NHS figures show that almost two-thirds of the British population are categorised as either over-weight or obese – 67% of men and 62% of women.[40] While carrying a little extra weight is rarely regarded as highly harmful, a rising (and alarming) number of us are heading into unhealthy territory. If you think that might include you, here are some facts to con-sider when it comes to your health.

Being overweight or obese can have a serious impact on health. 'Carrying extra fat', says the World Health

---

40 Lifestyles Team, NHS Digital (2019) 'Statistics on Obesity, Physical Activity and Diet, England, 2019'. www.digital.nhs.uk/data-and-information/publications/statistical/statistics-on-obesity-physical-activity-and-diet/statistics-on-obesity-physical-activity-and-diet-england-2019/part-3-adult-obesity

Organisation, 'leads to serious health consequences such as cardiovascular disease (mainly heart disease and stroke), Type 2 diabetes, musculoskeletal disorders like osteoarthritis, and some cancers (endometrial, breast and colon).'[41]

The Government recommends that men consume 2,500 calories a day and women 2,000 calories – which is way below the guidelines in the 1940s.[42] World War Two rations were designed to provide 3,000 calories a day, and people actually lost weight if they got less than 2,900 calories a day.

Despite increasing amounts of labelling, keeping tabs on calorie intake is never easy – especially if we live a busy life. Ironically, being 'busy' doesn't always equate to burning energy. Calories out have to match calories in, and since the 1960s, physical activity has declined by 24%.[43] Over time, even a modest surplus each day can soon add up. The only way we can measure this is by weighing ourselves regularly. So, what are 'healthy weights' for us to target?

41 World Health Organization (2013) 'What Are The Health Consequences of Being Overweight?' www.who.int/features/qa/49/en
42 J. M. Harries and D. F. Hollingsworth (1953) 'Food Supply, Body Weight, and Activity in Great Britain, 1943–9', *Br Med J.*, Jan 10; 1(4801): 75–78. www.ncbi.nlm.nih.gov/pmc/articles/PMC2015221
43 Public Health England (2014) 'Everybody Active, Every Day: Framework for Physical Activity'. www.gov.uk/government/publications/everybody-active-every-day-a-framework-to-embed-physical-activity-into-daily-life

The most common method applied these days is Body Mass Index (BMI), which is calculated as weight (in kilograms) divided by height (in metres) squared. So, someone who weighs in at 100 kilograms and is 1.8 metres high has a BMI of 100 divided by 1.8 x 1.8 = 30.86kg/m². This person's BMI is approximately 31kg/m².

According to this method,[44] if your BMI is:

- Below 18.5 – you're underweight

- Between 18.5 and 24.9 – you're in the healthy weight range

- Between 25 and 29.9 – you're overweight

- Between 30 and 39.9 – you're in the obese range

- Forty or above means you're severely obese

Another way of looking at it is this: men with a waist circumference of 94 cm (37 in) or more are at increased risk of health problems, while women with a waist circumference of 80 cm (31.5 in) or more are similarly at an increased risk of health problems.[45] There are limitations of the BMI, not least because it does not distinguish between muscle and fat, so most professional rugby players would find themselves being

---

44 NHS (2019) 'What is The Body Mass Index (BMI)?' www.nhs.uk/ common-health-questions/lifestyle/what-is-the-body-mass-index-bmi
45 NICE (2006) 'Obesity: full guidance'. www.nice.org.uk/guidance/ cg43/evidence/full-guideline-section-2-identification-and-classification-evidence-statements-and-reviews-pdf-195027230

categorised as overweight. This is where a set of scales which measures body fat and expresses it as a percentage of your total weight can provide a more accurate measurement.

All of us need a certain amount of fat in our body (described as 'essential fat'), but here are some helpful guidelines courtesy of the American Council on Exercise.[46]

Percent Body Fat Norms for Women and Men

Description	Women	Men
Essential fat	10–13%	3–5%
Athletes	14–20%	6–13%
Fitness	21–24%	14–17%
Average	25–31%	18–24%
Obese	32%+	25%+

A straightforward target would be to work out the percentage of body fat you'd like to lose and work out what that represents in kilos or pounds. If, for instance you weigh 80 kilograms and you want to go down by 5%, that's 80 x 0.5 to take off: 4 kilograms.

If you're going to cut your weight by reducing your calorie intake, one simple way is to reduce your alcohol intake. Remember that one pound of weight

---

46 Percent Body Fat Calculator. www.acefitness.org/education-and-resources/lifestyle/tools-calculators/percent-body-fat-calculator

represents 3,500 calories (7,700 calories for a kilogram). That's around seventeen pints of beer for a pound (thirty-seven for a kilogram). A bottle of wine is around 635 calories, so 5.5 bottles for a pound (twelve for a kilogram).

Prefer the fast food route to trim the fat? A Big Mac is 505 calories – so take seven of those out of your diet over a month and you'll be a pound to the good. A Costa Primo full milk latte packs 161 calories – go the espresso route for the next twenty-two days and lose a pound of unwanted baggage. You can find the impact on your body of all your fast food favourites here: www.nutracheck.co.uk/Home

If you prefer to combine your weight loss programme with some exercise, that will speed the process significantly: swimming, running and cycling can (depending on your weight and the intensity of the exercise) typically burn between 600 and 900 calories an hour;[47] walking can burn between 350 and 500 calories an hour. More than that, exercise will make your body work more efficiently, as well as lift your mood.

According to the helpful exercise advice section on the NHS website, to stay healthy, adults aged nineteen to sixty-four should try to be active daily and do:

---

47 Kirsten Nunez (2019) '12 exercises that burn the most calories'. www.healthline.com/health/what-exercise-burns-the-most-calories#calorie-burning-exercises

- At least 150 minutes of moderate aerobic activity such as cycling or brisk walking every week *and*

- Strength exercises on two or more days a week that work all the major muscles (legs, hips, back, abdomen, chest, shoulders and arms)

Or:

- Seventy-five minutes of vigorous aerobic activity such as running or a game of tennis every week *and*

- Strength exercises on two or more days a week that work all the major muscles (legs, hips, back, abdomen, chest, shoulders and arms)

Or:

- A mix of moderate and vigorous aerobic activity every week – for example, 2 x thirty-minute runs plus thirty minutes of brisk walking equates to 150 minutes of moderate aerobic activity *and*

- Strength exercises on two or more days a week that work all the major muscles (legs, hips, back, abdomen, chest, shoulders and arms)

They also point out that one minute of vigorous activity provides the same health benefits as two minutes of moderate activity. Moderate activity will raise your heart rate, and make you breathe faster and feel warmer. Vigorous activity makes you breathe hard and fast. If you're working at this level, you won't be able to say more than a few words without pausing for breath. At the former, the so-called 'speed of chat' in running parlance, you'll be able to converse at the same time.

There is plenty of research to show that the best combination of exercise as you get older is to combine strength training with cardio – building up your muscles as well as keeping your heart and lungs working. It needn't be a chore, but it does need to be consistent, and ideally enjoyable too. You don't have to don the Lycra, become a gym bunny or pound the streets: a 2017 study by Swim England found that those who swim regularly have a 28% lower risk of early death and a 41% lower risk of death as a result of stroke or heart disease,[48] while brisk walking can also be highly effective. According to a study published in the *British Journal of Sports Medicine*, walking for just ten to fifty-nine minutes per week or even gardening can lower the risk of death from any cause by 18%.[49]

48 British Swimming (2017) 'Major New Study on Health Benefits of Swimming Released'. www.britishswimming.org/news/general-swimming-news/major-new-study-health-benefits-swimming-released

49 BMJ (2019) 'Even Low Levels of Leisure Time Physical Activity Lowers Risk of Death'. www.bmj.com/company/newsroom/even-low-levels-of-leisure-time-physical-activity-lowers-risk-of-death

Monitoring your health

Once you reach the age of forty you qualify for an NHS Health Check.[50] This is a five-yearly event, but a pharmacy or your local GP will always conduct the basic tests if you ask them to: weight, heart rate, blood pressure, blood sugar and cholesterol level. While healthy readings are no guarantee of you being in full health, they will often flag up underlying conditions or the need to change your lifestyle. Perhaps surprisingly, an examination of your eyes by your optometrist can also act as an early indicator for conditions such as high blood pressure, diabetes and even tumours.

For the purpose of having a thorough overhaul of your wellbeing as part of an MLR, you might consider going to a private health provider: for anything from a couple of hundred pounds upwards you will get a full 'service'. It might seem expensive, but the alternative of not acting on an underlying condition could prove more serious in the long-term.

What does 'healthy' look like when boiled down to basic numbers? Here are some to take on board.

Blood pressure

This is a measure of the force that your heart needs to pump blood around your body – and will indicate a

---

50 NHS Health Check. www.nhs.uk/conditions/nhs-health-check

range of conditions, especially if the reading is higher than it ideally should be. One in four adults suffer from high blood pressure, and this contributes to over 75,000 deaths a year.[51] It can usually be reduced with changes in lifestyle and medication.

Blood pressure is given as two figures:

- Systolic pressure (when your heart pushes blood out around your body)

- Diastolic pressure (when your heart is resting)

For example, if your blood pressure is '130 over 80', you have a systolic pressure of 130mmHg and a diastolic pressure of 80mmHg.

- High blood pressure is 140/90mmHg or above

- Ideal blood pressure is between 90/60mmHg and 120/80mmHg

- Low blood pressure is 90/60mmHg or lower

There is more information available here: www.nhs.uk/ common-health-questions/lifestyle/what-is-blood-pressure.

---

51 NICE (2019) 'Thousands Set To Benefit From Blood Pressure Treatment Under New NICE Guidance'. www.nice.org.uk/news/article/ thousands-set-to-benefit-from-blood-pressure-treatment-under-new-nice-guidance

Cholesterol

It would be easy to find yourself confused about how healthy – or unhealthy – high levels of cholesterol are or what sort of foods to avoid. Reports and research providing seemingly contradictory evidence appear in the media on a regular basis. It doesn't help that there are deemed to be two types of cholesterol – one of which is good for you, the other not so. In addition, while having too much of the 'wrong' cholesterol is often the result of poor lifestyle and diet, it can also be genetic.

That makes it even more important to have your levels checked – even if you think you're doing all the right things. Too much cholesterol can block your blood vessels and increase the likelihood of heart problems or a stroke. High cholesterol does not necessarily cause symptoms, so it can build up over time without you being aware. You can only find out if you have an unhealthy reading by a taking a blood test. Your low-density lipoproteins (LDL) or 'bad' cholesterol score should be three or less, and your total cholesterol five or less. Again, you can take steps to reduce an unhealthily high level of cholesterol in your blood through diet, exercise and medication.

Pulse rate

While all heart rates differ, and your own heart rate will also vary depending upon what level of activity you are undertaking, most adults have a resting heart rate between 60 and 100 beats per minute (bpm). If yours is higher than that it is well worth checking to see if you have any underlying health problems. If it is lower than forty and you are not an athlete, it can also be worth checking.

You can check your own pulse in your wrist or neck – something worth doing as you are exercising or recovering from exercise to check you are not overdoing it or to see how your fitness regime is going. There is more information here to help you: www.nhs.uk/common-health-questions/accidents-first-aid-and-treatments/how-do-i-check-my-pulse.

Top tips for getting and staying fit in your midlife onwards

Everyone will have a different outlook on exercise – while some will embrace it, others will do anything to avoid it. You also have to go at your own pace if you are to avoid undoing any health benefits by tearing muscles, damaging joints or over-exerting your heart. But the right sort of exercise, undertaken regularly, will not only help you retain a healthy body, it can be great for the mind too. Speaking from experience, the endorphin rush you get after a long run or bicycle ride is one of life's great (and cheapest) pleasures. You sleep better, have more energy, and it gives you a little extra scope for an occasional treat.

Look to build flexibility exercises into your routine as well – strengthening muscles is great but stretches will make sure you continue to have a full range of movement as you get older. Pilates, yoga or Tai Chi can be as gentle or as rigorous as you choose and are great ways to keep you supple, as well as relax you and help put your mind and body back into balance.

Here are some suggestions to assist you:

- If you are taking up a new exercise, check with your doctor. I had a thorough check before I undertook my first marathon and that gave me the confidence to train and enjoy (sort of!) the experience itself.

- Do something you enjoy and that matches your body type. If you don't, you'll soon get demotivated or develop injuries.

- Don't overdo it, especially at the beginning. If you really want to run, for instance, and you're carrying a lot of weight, try losing some through cycling, rowing in the gym or dieting before you put excess strain on your joints.

- Set yourself targets – nothing too adventurous, but it's great to see your times coming down or your distances going up steadily. You'll be amazed how quickly you improve when you start.

- Make time for your exercise and write it in your diary. Look upon it as your 'reward' for a hard day at work. In short, make it a priority.

- Join a gym. There are several good reasons why: first, having paid your membership, you'll feel guilty if you aren't getting your money's worth; second, there is a variety of ways to stay fit, so you can vary your routine and make sure you get a mix of weights and cardio exercise; and third, when it's a wet February night, you won't find yourself making excuses about going for a run – a gym is always warm and dry.

FIVE

Planning The Rest Of Your Career

Midlife is the perfect time to pause and reflect on where you'd like to be over the next ten or twenty years, and this case study typifies what can come out of that – with the right employee and employer.

JAMES' STORY

James is fifty-two. Like many of his generation, he's only been with two employers since leaving university: first in the public sector as a public relations assistant and then moving into the marketing department of a large company. Over the last twenty-five years he has steadily moved up the ladder, reaching the post of Marketing Director for one of their divisions.

Being part of a generous DB pension scheme, he knows that when he reaches fifty-five, he can (theoretically) afford to take early retirement, albeit this would mean living a far more frugal life than at present. He also has the second of his two children about to go to university, and he is keen to provide her with as much financial assistance as he did for his first child. His wife Jan is working part-time in the pensions sector after returning ten years ago; much of the rest of her time is spent caring for her elderly father who lives alone in a retirement complex a few miles away.

In James' words:

'Last year, Jan and I managed to get a long holiday together – the first we'd spent with just the two of us since before the children were born – and we ended up having long chats about where we both go from here. We'd never really done that before – for years, we'd just got on with paying the bills and bringing up the kids.

I reached the conclusion that, while I still enjoyed my work, it had some major downsides. There was a lot of travelling – not just commuting but often to exhibitions and trade fairs, and that can pall after a while! The salary was good, but I knew I didn't need to earn it all in order to live the life we wanted. And I knew that Jan could do with a hand sometimes with her dad. I also fancied getting out on my bike a bit more often.

So, I felt that some sort of change at work would be good – but I didn't want a role that was just 'coasting' until I retired. I still feel at the top of my game, I still want a challenge. Through her work Jan had read about the concept of a Midlife MOT or career review, and while my employers didn't run anything quite like that, the annual review does offer the opportunity to have an in-depth discussion if that is what you want. I asked my line manager if we could have just that – a frank chat looking at the next five or ten years.

My line manager was really open to talking about my future career and we sat down with HR to do just that. Beforehand though, I took financial advice from an independent financial adviser (IFA) who set out all the figures for me – how much I needed to save to make sure I could retire comfortably. That was money well spent as I also ended up transferring the pension pot from my first employer to one that offered higher returns and lower charges.

I also took the opportunity to have a thorough health check through my private health provider – something else recommended in the literature I'd read. The check picked up that I was quite close to the top of the ideal cholesterol level and that I needed to shed a few kilos that had somehow crept on without me noticing, but nothing that an uptick in exercise wouldn't fix. That was actually reassuring as several friends of mine have had major ops in their fifties out of the blue. A pressured job and too many late nights at trade fairs can do that to you.

What came out of the discussion was far better than I'd hoped. They started off by saying they were keen to keep me in the company, which is a good place to begin. They were particularly concerned about the number of senior personnel who had left over the past few years and weren't keen to lose more. I set out my main objectives: to work fewer hours and do less travelling while still having a challenging role.

What came out of that was a suggestion that I take on a mentoring role to younger members of the marketing teams throughout the business. Not all line managers have the time to provide oversight to those coming up through the ranks and we'd lost several really promising people because of that.

This meant me undertaking some training to get up to speed on some of the disciplines I'd always delegated before – like social media, webinars and video production – as well as learning more about mentoring itself. That offered me some real opportunities to keep learning, and I could cut my working hours by a day a week starting immediately – and review that in the future. I could easily afford that reduction in salary and I would still be making contributions to my pension.

We touched on when I might like to stop work. Really, I'm not sure – but we have now booked in annual reviews to keep that option open. It's been a real win-win for my company and I and they are now looking to offer similar reviews to other people in their fifties and sixties.'

SIX

The Workplace Conversation

Why today could be the start of the rest of your career

The 'third leg' of the MLR stool is 'work'. If, like James in the case study above, you think – having assessed your finances and your wellbeing – that you'd like to make changes to your role (now or in the future) an MLR can be your opportunity.

Before speaking to an employer though, it's well worth considering all of your options – ideally knowing the financial implications of each of them, to build a picture of what the trajectory of your future career might look like. It's often assumed that a 'given' of the MLR is that the employee will be wanting to wind down or to move sideways. Not true. It may well be that you think you have skills that are not being recognised and harnessed, or that you feel overlooked: this could be the chance to discuss those thoughts. It is also worth considering is the impact this might have for your employer: the benefits as well as potential drawbacks of harnessing your skills in a different role going forward.

The other aspect for you to deliberate upon is updating your skills to meet new and future demands within the organisation: this will be something they will certainly be offering younger employees but may not necessarily assume that older employees will be as open to training. Finally, if you are looking to make adjustments because of care responsibilities, check your contractual rights as well as your statutory ones – some employers do offer more generous rights than they are legally obliged to do. Some offer paid as well as unpaid leave.

Having a conversation with your employer as part of an MLR doesn't necessarily mean either of you are looking to make changes in the short or even long-term. Indeed, in an ideal world, employers and employees wouldn't see the MLR as a one-off exercise, and certainly not one only undertaken with a view to making changes. Enlightened employers like Aviva are making these an annual exercise which allows an employer or line manager to better understand the individual's personal circumstances (as far as they affect their work) as well as their career concerns and ambitions – a platform to make small adjustments to a person's trajectory and working conditions to avoid major changes becoming necessary further down the line; for example, an employee leaving due to personal pressures.

One in nine of the workforce are caring for someone who is older, disabled or seriously ill in this country, who already try and combine their work with care responsibilities. As many again have given up work to look after a loved one – a huge loss to the individuals, their employers and the national economy.[52] This figure is set to rise significantly in the years to come as six hundred people each week continue to leave work to care for a relative, making the MLR a critical strategic resource in helping employers and employees to find solutions. This is how a frank and open conversation between an employee and her employer allowed her to keep earning – and caring.

SALLY'S STORY

Sally, now fifty-four, joined her present company ten years ago. She is a qualified IFA providing pensions and financial advice to individuals and small business owners from a regional branch office.

Her mother started showing signs of dementia five years ago but, until recently, was largely able to manage her home as well as care for her husband (who has Parkinson's), with Sally dropping in on her way to and

---

52 www.employersforcarers.org/about-us; Tim Smedley (2012) 'Have a Care for the Carers Forced to Give Up Work', *Guardian*. www.theguardian.com/money/2012/jun/29/carers-forced-give-up-work

from work each day. Her younger sister, who lives forty miles away, takes over care duties on the weekends.

The solution Sally came up with to achieve a less stressful life/work balance involved asking her employer if she could work flexibly. This concept is explored in greater depth in a later section, but the key point to bear in mind is that employees have the right to ask for greater flexibility and should ideally go to their employers with ideas on how they can accommodate that.

In Sally's words:

'We always knew that the situation was only ever going to become more difficult as time went on, but all of us have pulled together and made it work for as long as we could. The time had come for moving into a different gear, but that posed problems.

I couldn't really afford to give up my job, and nor could my sister, but neither could the family afford to pay for the care our parents needed if things got worse. They have a modest amount of savings, so they don't qualify for free care – but we all wanted to keep that money intact in case one of them ever needed to go into care. Bit of a catch-22.

When my sister rang to say that she'd arrived one Sunday morning to find my mother had left the house and was wandering the neighbourhood when she got there, we both knew the situation was unsustainable. We didn't want to put our parents into a care home but how could we provide the extra care they needed?

I knew about MLRs from an article I'd read in the financial press and started doing some research. My company is too small to have gone down this road, but they are one of the more 'enlightened' employers around and so

I thought I'd ask them if we could have a conversation – with no commitment on either side – on what I might do to keep earning a living but reduce my workload.

They said they were keen to keep me and they'd be open to a more flexible arrangement but were concerned about how they would replace me if I radically reduced my hours or went part-time.

I worked out that we could get by financially with me going down to four days a week, and if I spent two half days working 'from home' I could actually work from my parents' house – and that would give me an extra day to keep an eye on them. My sister was able to talk to her boss (it helps that he is her brother-in-law) and she too could go down to four days a week.

Both of us had (fortunately) taken on lasting powers of attorney for the property and financial affairs of our parents and looked at taking out an equity release policy that allowed us to draw down up to £50,000 over the next five years. That would give us enough to fund someone coming in to provide cover for several hours on the two days when neither of us could be there between 9am and 6pm. Our parents – like all parents – had always been keen to pass on as much of their property wealth to us as they could, but that really took second place to ensuring they were cared for properly in their later years.

My sister's husband installed monitoring equipment which also linked both of us up, as well as extra smoke alarms and a detector that would flag up if mum left the house when we weren't there.

The final step was to discuss the details with my boss but I did plenty of homework before that. I knew that by installing broadband in my parent's house I could keep in touch with the office through Skype whenever necessary, as well as connect into the server remotely for client files and the software I needed. That covered one concern I knew he'd have. Next, I knew that one of our staff had been part-time for the last five years while her children were at junior school. We talked and she said she'd be more than willing to increase her hours given the opportunity.

Armed with that, I asked for an informal chat to talk about the issues I was facing and whether they would allow me to work four days a week, with the equivalent of one of those days working from home. As my boss said in the meeting, my value to the company was in the personal contacts I had built up in my time there. They had staff in other branches on similar arrangements and that had worked well. They could also cope with me working one day a week less.

Ultimately, there was no problem at all making the adjustments, and I found he was incredibly sympathetic to my situation, offering for me to adjust my working day if I needed to so I could avoid the traffic at either ends of the day.

I won't lie, it's hard work combining work and care, but I am actually far more on top of things now we've resolved the situation, and I'm not stressing about my parents so much, which (if I'm honest) was a big distraction at times. At some point, one or both of them may need to go into care and we'll think again – and I know the door will be open to me having another conversation with my employer.'

What can employees learn from this?

Sally's situation is similar to millions of other people in their middle years needing to make changes to achieve a work/life blend or balance that is sustainable to them and their employers. Her experience of negotiating changes to her employment contract was informed by the MLR, if not actually driven by it. The concept is still in its infancy and hasn't really entered the SME arena as yet, but her example demonstrates what can be achieved if the key elements are in place:

- The employee needs to look at their personal situation in the round – including the financial impact any changes might make.

- The employee should also try and consider any request for changes from the employer's perspective, and if they can come to the conversation with solutions to any problems that might crop up, that will be helpful.

- It's important to consider whether this is a short, medium or long-term situation and to build in the possibility of further conversations should circumstances change. Look on it as a 'process' – not a one-off discussion.

Here are a few things with which to 'gird' yourself before you enter an MLR conversation. Looking at your current work/life balance, do you want to:

- Work fewer hours?

- Do the same number of hours but reconfigure them?

- Take on a less demanding role?

- Change roles to make better use of the skills you have acquired?

- Combine care responsibilities with your paid work?

- Travel less/more in your work?

- Work more from home?

- Receive training to reskill yourself?

- Build a mentoring role into your work?

- Take a sabbatical to recharge your batteries?

- Reduce your commitments to do voluntary work?

- Reduce your commitments to set up a new venture?

Importantly, you need to have considered:

- What impact might any changes make on your employer's business?

- Have you any ideas on how any potential negative impacts might be reduced?

- Are there ways in which your employer can benefit from any changes?

- What level of salary will you need to receive going forwards to meet your financial objectives?

- What salary adjustment is your employer likely to propose?

- Is this a realistic adjustment from your perspective?

- What impact might any changes make on your pension and any other company benefits, such as a company car?

- Is this a short-term proposal to cover an emergency that may resolve itself in the future? (If so, your discussion should focus on the length of time you might need to reduce your hours or responsibilities.)

The discussion around salary and pensions

If, following an MLR review, you and your employer conclude that you need to take on a less onerous role in the business, expect there to be a discussion around salary.

This may also have implications for your pension – for both DB and DC types, making advice essential. Also bear in mind that a priority for you going forwards may well be boosting your pension rather than receiving all of your salary: this can be a highly tax efficient way to build your pension pot, as you will not be taxed on what you save up to the limit of £40,000 in a year.

In summary: wealth, work and wellbeing

From an employee's perspective, no MLR review can be conducted meaningfully unless you have all the information available to help map out your future.

From a financial perspective, you need to know:

1. Whether or not you are on track to save enough for a comfortable later life or retirement at a time of your choosing

2. What changes you need to make to achieve that, if that isn't the case

3. Whether you can afford to make any changes to your job or hours that would affect your income and future pension

From a health perspective, ensure that you have:

1. Assessed your physical and mental wellbeing

2. Recognised the impact this is having/could have on your work and life

3. Made conscious choices to make any changes you think would be beneficial

Armed with that, you can now have a conversation with your employer/line manager on whether there are health or personal circumstances – such as caring responsibilities, health issues or financial pressures – that that are making it difficult for you to work in the way you are currently being expected to.

If so, what changes might be beneficial? Consider factors such as to your:

- Hours
- Role
- Responsibilities
- Career prospects
- Training opportunities
- Working environment

There is no fixed template MLR that will suit every employer or employee, but if both sides go into the process looking to achieve a mutually reasonable and positive outcome then both sides will gain. The alternative is for valuable employees to potentially be lost to the workforce and for those individuals to face financial hardship or continue in untenable situations that could jeopardise their health and wellbeing.

PART TWO

THE EMPLOYER PERSPECTIVE

SEVEN

The Benefits Of Implementing A Midlife Review

Ask any of the organisations starting to integrate an MLR into their workplace practices what got them started and there is a common reply: quite simply, it makes business sense.

To date, it has almost entirely been larger corporates that have recognised that they face major future challenges if they don't put in place a mechanism to stop talented people walking out off the door at a time of *their* choosing, simply because they haven't bothered to have a conversation which flagged up their employees' needs, concerns and aspirations.

They recognise that the continuing drain of talent from their management structure will leave them lacking in the experience and skills that older personnel bring.

For many bigger businesses it's meant a radical reversal in policy because early redundancy has actually been encouraged in the past to free up routes to the top for younger personnel, and that has been facilitated by the generous DB pensions that many larger corporates provide.

SMEs won't necessarily be facing the same issues, so what's in it for them?

Most organisations will already conduct regular reviews with their personnel. Where the MLR adds far more value is the depth of detail it goes into, together with the potential to join up the dots between a person's work and personal life.

A standard review won't provide the sort of information on their finances and wellbeing that will allow them to come to an informed decision on when, for instance, they can afford to retire or wind down work. It won't tell them how much more they need to tuck away in their pension pot. Neither will it necessarily open up a conversation around the other pressures in their lives that are negatively impacting them.

A process that encourages individuals to reflect on all aspects of their lives provides an opportunity for employers to have a wide ranging discussion that will allow the company to plan for the longer term as well as make the most of their staff resources.

Quite possibly the most important condition for any MLR conversation is that both parties understand that it is not a formal discussion binding on either side, but informal and without prejudice. This avoids the potential for a suggestion, for instance, by an employer to an employee that they leave or reduce their hours because of their age or care responsibilities to be regarded as discriminatory. Any solution arrived at in an MLR can be formally agreed at a later date.

The employer must also recognise that an employee will be anxious about discussing changes to their working arrangements if they feel this will be a pre-text for an employer to regard them as not committed to the business and use that as a context for demoting them or making them redundant. Unless this trust exists, the MLR has no value and could, potentially, be harmful to the employee/employer relationship. Certainly, any employer who does use the process in a way that could be perceived as discriminatory or unfair would scupper the possibility of other staff ever repeating the exercise.

Key benefits of implementing MLRs

What, then are the key benefits which you, as an employer, can hope to achieve through implementing the MLR with your staff? Here are a few to consider, together with examples of how they could work in practice.

It's a well-worn cliché that your people are your biggest asset, but are you really making the most of them? Older personnel may well occupy an important position within the business – but how long have they been there? Are they just treading water, and have you ever considered that their skills and experience might be better utilised elsewhere?

Let's see how applying this principle within an MLR might look in practice:

PHILIP: MAXIMISATION OF TALENT

Philip has been with the business for twenty-two years running the accounts department. He's fifty-four now and probably reached as high within the company's ranks as he's going to get – middle management. That said, he's one of the lynch pins of the business: customers know and trust him; younger staff turn to him for advice; the Finance Director see him as his eyes and ears in accounts.

Philip has always had a regular career review, but it has rarely gone into any depth on how he feels about his future with the company. His boss knows he's settled – but what more does he need to know? Philip's MLR revealed some important and unexpected information: he feels comfortable in his present role, but feels that it has stopped presenting the challenges that once made each day different. In particular, he's concerned that he hasn't done any training for over ten years, even though the personnel below him have. He's worried that he's going to get left behind as the company takes on new systems, and he certainly won't be in a position to advise younger personnel. That makes his position in the business vulnerable. After looking at his personal finances, it's clear that he needs to work at least another ten years in order to retire comfortably. He wants to make sure he will still be relevant to the company during that time.

As a result of Philip's MLR, he has now been put on a series of training programmes to update his skills (the Finance Director had not even considered him for more training previously, assigning the courses to younger personnel instead). The company has also formalised the role he plays advising younger personnel by creating an additional mentoring responsibility that puts all new recruits under his wing for their first twelve months. Both Philip and his employer have gained significantly out of the process.

CAROLINE: RETENTION OF KEY PERSONNEL

Caroline's employer is a small, specialist manufacturer and she has been with them for some eighteen years – first helping to set up their IT system, then taking on the role of overseeing their parts procurement and overseas sales. She is an important 'cog', with key information about the business, its processes and its clients at her fingertips.

Her MLR highlighted something her employer had not appreciated: at fifty-five, Caroline still needs to keep earning for at least another ten to twelve years, but her life is coming under increasing pressure because her mother has been diagnosed with Alzheimer's. While she is just about managing at the moment, she may well need to spend increasing amounts of her time making sure that her mother and her elderly father are looked after and safe. She has been actively considering leaving and taking on a part-time job where she could have more flexibility.

Caroline's MLR led to her employer allowing her to go down to a six-hour day and set up a way for her to work remotely one afternoon a week. That has allowed Caroline to check in on her parents at the start and end of each day, as well as work from there when needed. Another member of staff is also being trained up to take on some of Caroline's responsibilities. This arrangement is to be under review in case the situation changes further.

JACK: RELEASING KEY PERSONNEL FOR OTHER ROLES

Jack was the oldest person in his company to be offered an MLR. At sixty-three, he had for some time made no secret of the fact that he was looking forward to kicking back in the not-too-distant future. He had been one of the company's top sales staff for over thirty years, and he had built an unrivalled knowledge of their products as well as a great network of valuable contacts. He still loved the craic of working with his colleagues and the buzz of landing a contract, but the endless overnight stays and motorway miles had long lost their charm.

His MLR financial assessment revealed that, while he had a reasonable private pension to rely upon, which he could take at any time, he wouldn't be receiving his state pension for another three years. When he added up the sums, he realised that he really did need to keep topping up his income until then.

His line manager came up with an offer that really suited both Jack and the company. The company attended around six trade events each year – four in the UK, two in Germany. These took out key members of the sales and technical teams for around a week each time. If Jack could take on the role of coordinating and managing those stands, as well as manning them, it would release valuable members of staff to undertake their other roles – a significantly better use of resources.

Jack's contract was renegotiated so that he started drawing his company pension and went self-employed with a guaranteed number of days working each year – which amounted to about a day each week. The company agreed to split his expected annual income into twelve equal parts, which helped him balance his incomings and outgoings. That more than covered the gap in his income, while allowing him to stay in touch with his friends and contacts and still improve his golf handicap in his days away from work.

STUART: FACILITATING SUCCESSION PLANNING

Since Stuart had become Chief Executive Officer (CEO) of a mid-sized IFA practice ten years previously, he had become increasingly conscious of the fact that his workforce was ageing: relatively few had left, and that had resulted in fewer opportunities to take on younger personnel. It had also made it difficult to promote some promising middle managers as quickly as they were hoping – and several had left to competitors as a result. Retaining the most talented of this 'layer' of staff was critical to the long-term future of the company, as among them were his best hopes for the future top management.

Offering the MLR to all staff over forty-five provided an opportunity for Stuart to set out a template for the future. Because of the sensitivity of some of the conversations, an outside consultant was brought in to handle the interviews, who worked in complete confidentiality. Right from the start, Stuart impressed upon his staff that there was no pressure on anyone to leave the business – in fact that was the opposite of what he wanted as he saw everyone as a valuable part of the operation. The conversations allowed him to identify the timescales in which his older personnel would like to wind down or retire, who would prefer to take on new roles, and who – given the opportunity – would reduce their hours or move to being part-time to achieve a better work/life balance.

This allowed him to make a series of strategic moves where several of the directors were assigned up-and-coming middle managers to shadow them and acquire the skills they would need to lead the business in the future, while several more changed branches and were promoted – with plans to bring them back into the main office at some point in the future.

A number of older personnel took the opportunity to go part-time, having been provided with financial advice on how much they would need to earn and save in the years ahead. The cost savings and role changes achieved also enabled Stuart to give a number of people a promotion and a pay rise.

The exercise acted as a major boost to the morale of his staff as they had already recognised the tensions within the business and were concerned that they might find themselves moved sideways without any say in the matter. They saw the MLR as an unthreatening way to shape their own futures.

There will always be concerns that MLR discussions will be franker if held with an outsider but Stuart's bringing in an outside consultant paid dividends in that respect and the trust that was established in the process means that future MLRs at the company will almost certainly now be held between the individuals, their line managers and Stuart.

Retaining older personnel: Renegade Generation perspective

Renegade Generation is a company with a mission to 'supercharge career options for over 40s and provide ageing workforce solutions to employers'. Over the last four years, the company's founders, Fiona Green and Caroline Bosher, have been advising a series of blue-chip companies on how to recruit and retain mature talent by adopting age-friendly workplace practices. Their five-stage model – from strategic thought leadership sessions and auditing age diversity within an organisation through to showcasing an organisation's age-friendliness – scrutinises the processes and culture that may be inhibiting mature talent from working for them. Once diagnosed, Renegade Generation works with organisations to improve their age diversity 'blind spots'.

Their experiences demonstrate the frequent 'disconnect', as they describe it, between employers recognising that 'something needs to be done' – and actually doing it. Implementing an age strategy including the MLR, they say, could play a big role in resolving that.

'Promoting yourself as an "age-friendly" employer is gaining traction,' says Caroline Bosher, 'but it's clear that some organisations keen to travel down this road still have a way to go. We developed a list of companies that were positioning themselves as an attractive place for mature staff to work – entering awards, being an exemplar for age-friendly employer practices such as flexible working and carer support, saying the right things in their employment statements and so on. But every time we went onto their careers page, the imagery would include most aspects of a diverse and inclusive workforce... except age. What sort of message does that send out?

We also found companies were doing fantastic things on the inside, but never told people about it. Quite simply, there is often a disconnect between the teams running the corporate and jobs website and HR.'

So, how many companies are fully aware of the need to embrace and harness the talents of older workers and have got their messaging right?

'It's a very mixed picture,' maintains Caroline. 'Age is the one critical element missing from 92% of Diversity and Inclusion (D&I) strategies.[53] People we speak to in D&I are aware that it's not being addressed properly due to lack of awareness and urgency across C-Suite Officers, including HR and CEOs.'

'For some companies, the key issues (lack of talent and loss of vital corporate knowledge) are not biting yet,' adds Fiona Green, 'so it's not a priority on the board agenda. However, because they aren't feeling the pain it doesn't mean they aren't losing out. They're simply not thinking through the bottom line. The squeeze on the availability of younger talent is resulting in an increase in recruitment costs and time to recruit. When a decade of corporate knowledge walks out of the door, the value is huge when considering the cost of reskilling and training of new employees.

In contrast, we're now talking to a long-established IT business about why and how to retain their mature workforce because they know they are about to lose a lot of people with experience and knowledge of legacy hardware and software that's not going to be easy to replace.

Often the problem is not having a consistent cross-company policy. Within a single organisation, one customer services team may be really keen to recruit older people to match their staff to their target audience, and another

---

53 Victoria A. Lipnic (2018) 'The State of Age Discrimination and Older Workers in the U.S. 50 Years After the Age Discrimination in Employment Act (ADEA)', US Equal Employment Opportunity Commission. www.eeoc.gov/eeoc/history/adea50th/report.cfm

team seeks to hang onto corporate knowledge held by older executives. In contrast to this, another team may be trying to move older people on.'

For Fiona, the issue 'is a matter of leadership'. 'We spend our time getting businesses to think through their age strategy across the whole organisational structure – looking at the issue through a complex lens, then creating a company-wide culture to ensure that everyone is on the same page.'

Where does the MLR fit into this?

'Maybe we have a blinkered view,' says Caroline, 'as we are only talking to organisations that are addressing this issue – the ones that see supporting an ageing workforce as a way of gaining a competitive edge. For them, the MLR can be an invaluable tool.

It can encourage meaningful dialogues at critical times. Some companies are already enabling these touchpoint conversations throughout someone's career – to discuss role changes, learning and development, etc. For them, it's an ongoing process. Others simply haven't got a clue.

Embracing flexible working is a good example. Some team leaders will resist that because they worry it will cause them problems or that it was never something that was part of their own working experience. But with technology, almost all jobs can now be done flexibly – making it work is down to the culture, and how much the company trusts its staff.

Employers have the opportunity, as part of the MLR, to let people within an organisation know how flexible working could work for them. Yes, it can present real challenges for a CEO because, on the one hand, you allow team leaders the freedom to run things their way – however, that can cause conflict across teams. The infrastructure is often the barrier. Sales teams, for instance, may well have the infrastructure in place, but not other teams.

Organisations have to invest in the necessary equipment and systems, then support that with training and awareness.'

Retraining or upskilling is another area where employers need to take the lead, says Caroline, not least because older staff will assume they won't be offered the chance – even to the point of giving away the opportunities to younger staff.

'When we conduct our age audit, we analyse who is being offered access to learning and the age profile of the employees who access the learning opportunities. In some businesses, employees have done very little retraining and upskilling because their work hasn't changed that much – so retraining is foreign to them. These employees need encouragement and support to continue learning. Some are lifelong learners.

Employers need to be aware of the types of learning styles and offer suitable learning opportunities.

The MLR can act as a catalyst – impelling employers and staff to have a conversation they otherwise wouldn't have. However, for it to work, an MLR has to be part of a company-wide culture – one which is open to flexibility, uptraining and reskilling. From the employee's perspective they need some level of confidence going into that process.

In many instances, there's scope for specialist outsiders to act as a buffer: a fifty-seven year old going into a conversation with a younger line manager might not always go smoothly. This role can represent the good use of an older or former employee – someone who understands the company and the sector as well as the individual's perspective.'

The Centre for Ageing Better perspective

An organisation right at the heart of analysing research into MLRs is the Centre for Ageing Better. Their Evidence Manager, Aideen Young has been playing a key role to see what approaches work, and assessing the benefits in implementing reviews for a business, as well as for employees. Their full report on the research to date, compiled by Patrick Thomson, can be found on the link below.[54]

'I've been managing a project called "Transitions in Later Life" which has its origins in work on resilience carried out by experts such as Guy Robertson,' says Aideen Young. 'Resilience is a key attribute that helps us negotiate and adapt to significant sources of stress such as the "life transitions" that become more common from midlife onwards. What's really important in the context of our work on the MLR is that this vital quality – resilience – can actually be learned.

The Centre for Ageing Better partnered with the Calouste Gulbenkian Foundation (CGF) UK branch to evaluate two courses – one run by the Cheshire & Wirral NHS Trust and the other by Age and Opportunity in Dublin[55] – aimed at building resilience and helping prepare people to manage those challenging transitions. The courses use tools such as self-reflection, goal setting, mindfulness and CBT to help people take stock of their skills, relationships, character traits and personal philosophy while looking at approaches to transitions, ageing and ageism and physical, emotional and spiritual wellbeing.

---

54 Centre for Ageing Better (2018) 'Developing The Mid-Life MOT'. www.ageing-better.org.uk/sites/default/files/2018-09/Developing-the-mid-life-MOT.pdf
55 Calouste Gulbenkian Foundation (2018) 'Transitions in Later Life Learning Community'. www.gulbenkian.pt/uk-branch/transitions-later-life-learning-community-june-2018

We found that the courses resulted in improvement in wellbeing, attitudes to ageing and retirement, self-judgement and acceptance of change. But we also found that course participants became clearer about their goals for the future and went on to take some practical steps following the courses, including talking to family and friends about their plans for the future, seeking financial advice and speaking to their line managers about their working lives.

We are very concerned that people should plan and prepare for their later lives if those later lives are to be good; one of our earlier projects looked at the barriers and enablers of planning and found that those who most need to plan – the least advantaged among us – are least likely to do so.[56] We also know that people who don't plan for retirement tend to have worse outcomes.[57]

Our focus on the need for adequate planning and preparation for later life underpinned our interest in the MLR which, of course, led to our involvement in the pilot schemes run by Aviva, Legal & General, Mercer and the Pensions Advisory Service.

56 Centre for Ageing Better (2018) 'Planning and Preparing for Later Life'. www.ageing-better.org.uk/publications/planning-and-preparing-later-life

57 Centre for Ageing Better (2018) 'The Experience of the Transition to Retirement'. www.ageing-better.org.uk/publications/transition-to-retirement-rapid-evidence-review

Those pilot schemes identified health, wealth and self as the domains that should be addressed in an MLR. Following the results of our evaluation of the Transitions in Later Life courses, we think it's clear that psychological and emotional support should be included too. In fact, we think that the type of support offered by the types of courses evaluated could actually facilitate planning in the other domains. We see it as an essential component of the MLR, and that, in turn, is an essential part of being an age-friendly employer.'

THE COACH'S PERSPECTIVE: DANCING WITH FEAR AND CONFIDENCE

Laura Walker runs a consultancy called Midlife Careers, advising businesses as well as working with individuals making a significant career transition. Her own career includes senior roles within blue-chip businesses across six different sectors. Why does she focus on this cohort? Laura says:

'This is a demographic which faces unique challenges: they get less support than any other group of employees but they have the most potential to turn around their future lives. Indeed, there is a wealth of evidence which demonstrates that a minimal amount of support during midlife – providing an opportunity for them to pause and consider their future – makes all the difference.

However, within businesses, the advice, coaching and support that is made available for staff has historically tended to focus either on younger personnel or those about to retire. There's not always an awful lot going on for those in the middle. And yet midlife is a pivotal point – within our own lives, our families and the company: people in this age group are often the lynch pin, the quiet heroes holding it all together.

Why has there been this gap in support? In coaching we tend to promote the idea that we are all individuals, and so anything which "generalises" is seen as a dangerous sport but there are major themes around the challenges that many people face at this point in their lives. Ignoring these challenges hasn't proved particularly helpful.

It's also been a question of priorities for businesses. There's lots of talk in HR around the "future capabilities" that the company needs, and the consequences of that for technology, people skills, infrastructure and so on. That leads on to the question of who you choose to develop those capabilities. Many companies simply haven't bothered with employees past a certain age, preferring to invest in their future by concentrating on younger people; businesses are only now waking up to the idea that their future employees are already employed. Certainly, you will get more traction from speaking to the CEO, rather than HR, if they recognise that their business is hurting because they are losing staff – it also helps if you have a CEO prepared to try something new. Aviva are a good example of that.

I would say that the business case and the individual case for the MLR are the most compelling I've seen for interventions because it works for both perspectives. There's loads of evidence that you can turn around your life as an individual if you do something at this stage – between the ages of forty-five and sixty. But there can be inbuilt barriers – not least the fact that because there haven't been many training and coaching opportunities for this age cohort, older staff themselves don't expect to receive it and don't push for it. It therefore becomes a self-fulfilling expectation.

In addition, there is a naivete and denial around how long we are going to be working for. Plus, the ageism rife in society does affect individuals: the expression I use in my work of "dancing with fear and confidence" came out of my own research into the fascinating interplay between those two emotions when older people approach the topic of career reinvention.

That "fear" can be anything from a fear of "becoming my parents", becoming irrelevant or of slowing down. That last one is common, but it is a myth that we gradually slow down in later life; in fact, it is usually a series of discrete incidents which happen to individuals at different stages, and the pace of ageing varies between people. Moreover, your ability to learn is simply different – it's not any slower, better or worse than that of younger people. You just go about the process of learning differently.

Elliott Jacques has a lot to answer for by inventing the negative phrase "midlife crisis" which has been used as a shorthand for a point in life where one's powers are waning. Historically, midlife wasn't seen in that negative a way.[58] The work/life balance is often referred to, but I prefer talking about the "blend" in their lives, rather than the balance: the mix between the other aspects of their lives.

---

58 Elliott Jacques (1965) 'Death and the Mid-Life Crisis', *International Journal of Psychoanalysis* XLVI, p502–514.

There are countless stories of older people who have changed their lives around, and while they can be instructive, they can also be a bit dangerous. When people talk about changing what they do with their work, it is often more about their relationship with work rather than the content: how they feel about work and themselves, so more of an identity shift than a change of role.'

EIGHT

Flexible Working

In order for staff to achieve a better work/life blend, the potential for flexible working should be a key component of any MLR. Why is this becoming increasingly important – and how can flexibility benefit employers as well as employees?

There was a time when you could virtually set your watch by when the vast majority of staff – office as well as shop floor – clocked in to and out of work. Work hours were rigidly maintained and monitored. Taking time out for a 'sabbatical' or career break signalled a lack of ambition. Retirement was a cliff edge.

It was not until 1990 – fifteen years after the UK introduced its first maternity leave legislation through the Employment Protection Act 1975 – that all working women qualified. Previously, only about half of working women were eligible because of long qualifying periods of employment. It was only in 2003 that paid statutory paternity leave was extended to male employees.

Over the last decade or so, arguably the biggest single change within the workplace has been how many employers are now prepared to offer (varying degrees of) flexibility. This has really mattered to a growing number of employees of all ages for a variety of reasons – flexibility can allow them to vary their start and finish times, shorten their working day to care for dependents, go part-time, share a job with a colleague or even take a sabbatical.

It has enabled many of us to achieve a better work/life balance. It has also been a significant factor in helping more people to be economically active: in October 2019, the UK employment rate was estimated at 75.9%[59], just below its highest ever figure of 76.1% recorded in March of that year. In 2010, it hovered around the 70% mark.

Mercer's Global Talents Survey 2017[60] shows that 51% of UK employees across the age divide want more fluid work options, but what's in it for the employer? Should they feel obliged to say 'yes' if someone

---

59 Office For National Statistics (nd) 'Unemployment'. www.ons. gov.uk/employmentandlabourmarket/peoplenotinwork/ unemployment

60 Mercer (nd) 'Mercer Global Talent Trends Study 2017: UK results' (infographic). www.uk.mercer.com/our-thinking/global-talent-hr-trends.html

asks for more flexible working, and just how do you establish the trust that makes this beneficial to both employer and employee without becoming a potential source of tension?

One way to look at the concept of flexible working is as a useful 'pressure valve'. Most of us have to hold down a job and all of us need to live lives outside of that, but our lives cannot always be divided into conveniently labelled blocks of time. We have loved ones to care for, relationships to maintain, activities and pursuits that help define us for who we are, and health limitations.

Without the ability to have a level of flexibility – to take off an hour here or a half day there or to perhaps work alternative hours, some people's lives would be impossible. They would end up having stress-related illnesses, upping sticks to a more accommodating employer or even leaving the workforce altogether.

At a time when employers called all the shots, the 'my way or the highway' approach might have held sway, but we are not in that situation at present and talented people hold more of the bargaining chips. More to the point, the huge cost of recruiting and training those people and then bringing them up to speed (estimated in 2014 at £30,000)[61] makes retention a top management priority.

---

61 HR Review (2014) 'It Costs Over 30k To Replace A Staff Member'. www.hrreview.co.uk/hr-news/recruitment/it-costs-over-30k-to-replace-a-staff-member/50677

The 2017 CIPD 'Resourcing and Talent Planning'[62] report presciently set the scene for where we are now: 'Looking forward, organisations anticipate the biggest changes in the next three years will be increasing competition for well-qualified talent, developing existing staff and difficulty recruiting senior and skilled employees. It is therefore more important than ever that organisations remain alert to the potential changes and agile in their response to these in order to continue to attract and retain people with the best skills and potential for their business needs.'

In my last book, *Manage the Gap*, I set out how flexibility has become a cornerstone of employing younger employees. Their desire to achieve a better work/ life balance than previous generations has helped to drive flexibility as a key factor in recruiting as well as attracting and retaining talented Millennials and Gen Zs. This is a generation that has no plans to make their lives all about work. According to research carried out in July 2019 by Wildgoose, two in five younger employees plan to improve their mental health by moving to a company with flexible working.[63] They also have a far less defined boundary between work and the rest of their lives – they're quite happy to work at weekends or in the evenings if it means they

62 CIPD (2017) 'Resourcing and Talent Planning 2017'. www.cipd. co.uk/Images/resourcing-talent-planning_2017_tcm18-23747.pdf
63 Employer News (2019) 'UK Employees Moving to Flexible Workplaces to Improve Mental Health'. https://employernews.co.uk/ flexible-working/uk-employees-moving-to-flexible-workplaces-to-improve-mental-health

can take time out when they want or need to during normal office hours.

In Wildgoose's survey of workers aged forty-five or under, 14.3% of employees not currently allowed to work flexibly said that they are actively considering a career move to an organisation that would offer them flexible working. This figure goes up to 21% of parents in the same situation. The survey also reveals that a staggering 62% of employees have taken days off in the past year for mental health reasons, and if employers are serious about supporting mental health in the workplace, enabling flexible working to achieve a better work/life balance is a good place to start.

The availability of flexible working to achieve a better work/life balance is just as important to recruiting and retaining older workers. They will particularly appreciate the opportunity to squeeze in care responsibilities or in some cases, reduce their hours to slow the pace somewhat. Not accustomed to this expectation, they will often assume that it's not available as an option. They won't necessarily ask their employer about greater flexibility when it can often be the very thing that would allow them to carry on in a job they would otherwise have to leave.

This is not helped by line managers who are distrustful of flexibility because it hasn't been part of their workplace experience, combined with HR departments reluctant to write these policies into contracts because of the fear that new employees will take advantage of them, but there are lots of ways in which you can turn flexible working to your own advantage as well as for recruiting and retaining talented older workers – for instance, offering flexibility for personnel prepared to cover peak periods, and enabling 'agile working' to reduce your workspace requirements through sharing desks or offices.

Yes, it will mean compromises. Certainly, it will require planning and possibly changing some processes. It might even call for some investment in systems and equipment. It also has to be rolled out realistically: some departments and operations will need to approach it differently simply because they function in diverse ways. From my own experience though, you need to meet flexibility in the workplace head on: proactively rather than reactively.

The absolute minimum required of you by law is that you will consider a request for flexible working from a member of staff who has been with you for at least twenty-six weeks. By recognising that you potentially stand to benefit from introducing it, you can go much further and make it a powerful HR recruitment and retention tool, and that is why it has to be an integral part of any MLR review.

What do we mean by flexible working?

In fact, there are a number of options: so which ones could *your* business comfortably accommodate?

Flexitime: probably the best-known type, where employees fit their working hours either side of core office times. This is a good option for staff wishing to avoid lengthy and/or expensive rush hour commutes or parents doing the school run. It can also be helpful for those older staff who need to fit in care responsibilities at either end of the day – looking in on elderly relatives, for instance, or even doing the school run themselves for their grandchildren (this is, after all, the cohort often described as the 'sandwich generation'). Making it work for you will rely on having sufficient staff available to handle customer-facing duties at all times.

Annualised hours: here an employee has a contract to work a set number of hours across the year to suit their employer's needs. This will fit in well with employees who don't have specific obligations away from work – such as care responsibilities – but simply want to enjoy a better work/life blend. Annualised hours can also help employers who have peak or seasonal periods of work to manage, avoiding the need to recruit temporary and possibly inexperienced labour.

Restructured hours: compressing the working week so employees can, for example, do a nine-hour, four-day week. This will allow them to enjoy a better work/ life balance, take on care roles for family members during their spare days or even undertake training or upskilling. This can prove helpful for employers who have peak activity days, and also if they are trying to accommodate more personnel than they technically have space for – so an excellent way to introduce agile working.

It can also lead to a (perhaps surprising) boost in productivity. A recent study by Henley Business School saw 250 firms trying out a four-day week: nearly two-thirds of these businesses saw a productivity increase, as well as an improvement in their ability to recruit and retain staff. Between them, the companies taking part clocked up a boost of £92bn each year. Two-fifths of employees made use of their shorter working week to upskill.[64]

The research also found that 'this working style increased overall quality of life for employees, with over three-quarters (78%) of implementing businesses saying staff were happier, less stressed (70%) and took fewer days off ill (62%)'. Three-quarters of employees nationally, says the report, back a four-day working week – with 67% of Gen Zs saying 'it would drive them to pick a place to work'.

---

64 Henley Business School (2019) 'Four-day Week Pays Off for UK Business'. www.henley.ac.uk/news/2019/four-day-week-pays-off-for-uk-business

Home working: an increasingly popular option where employees work a certain number of half or full days out of the office. This can prove particularly helpful for staff who face long commutes, whose work would benefit from a quiet environment, or who need to be 'on hand' for relatives at certain times of the day. This practice probably requires the greatest level of faith from employers and line managers – but if you can't trust an employee, why did you take them on in the first place, especially if it is their output and results which matter most to you?

A prerequisite for many employees in this situation is a laptop with secure access to the company's server, and an ability to communicate through Skype or conference calls. Again, this allows companies to introduce cost-saving agile working. Many staff will also concentrate better when working away from a bustling environment if they have a major project to work on.

Reduced hours: for instance, going part-time or winding down for those looking to steadily reduce their work commitments. This will particularly help those who may no longer feel able or willing to work a full-time role, perhaps because of health reasons or care responsibilities. Part-time/reduced hour working allows businesses to retain the talents and experience of a valued member of staff on a reduced salary, as does letting someone taper towards retirement – giving you time to replace an employee as and when needed, or build up another employee's skills to fill that role, perhaps shadowing the senior member of staff.

Job-sharing: this can prove particularly helpful where two people are trying to cram in care responsibilities and can work flexibly together. It can often be a good working arrangement between an older worker and a parent who has to care for children in school holidays – as well as the odd inset day or when his or her child is poorly. These arrangements allow businesses to effectively retain two talents for the price of one, as well as provide cover during holidays and in the event of illness.

Career breaks/ sabbaticals: a gap year – a rarity in years gone by – is now commonplace for younger people, and increasingly popular among the older generation. And why not, after all those years with one's nose next to the grindstone? A break of a few months or more can be a perfect opportunity for someone to recharge their batteries, go on the pilgrimage or long-haul holiday they have always promised themselves before health becomes a consideration, help a family member through a serious illness, write a book, visit family abroad or (as in my case) take a second degree and go climbing in the Himalayas. From the employer's perspective, speaking from experience, it can mean retaining a valued team member who might otherwise suffer from burn-out. It can also provide the opportunity to test an up-and-coming younger talent in the office for a fixed period.

Your statutory obligations

Even if you don't have flexible working written into your HR policies as standard practices, since 2014 staff have had a statutory right to ask for flexible working arrangement: the Flexible Working Regulations that came into law that year also set out the minimum service eligibility criteria.[65] Those criteria include: the employee must have been working for the same employer for a minimum of twenty-six weeks; their request must be made in writing; and the request can only be made once a year. What's more, when they submit their application, the employee has to set out what effect they think it would have on the business.

Employers are allowed to say no, but they must deal with requests in a 'reasonable manner'. By that, the regulations set out as examples:

- Assessing the advantages and disadvantages of the application

- Holding a meeting to discuss the request with the employee

- Offering an appeal process

Speaking from experience, it's important to let prospective and existing staff clearly know your position on flexible working. That can often mean ensuring that

---

65 www.gov.uk/flexible-working

all your line managers share that information and that there is a cross-company understanding of how this should work. I have heard of many situations where resentment has built up in one department because staff in another are being seen to have a more congenial arrangement than theirs, leaving the CEO to pick up the pieces.

A company that manages the principle of flexibility proactively will be in better control of the process and avoid the possibility of staff leaving because they cannot cope with their current situation and difficulties recruiting talented people in a competitive environment. A companywide HR strategy built around flexibility lets everyone know where they stand (thus avoiding misunderstandings), allows managers to develop strategies for growth, and acts as the starting point for maximising the potential benefits of agile working.

Why flexibility should be in every MLR

Flexibility matters to most employees, but to older people it really can make a huge difference to their work/life balance. Aviva, the company leading the way nationally on midlife reviews, recently published research that showed why they are keen to support the carers in their company:[66] over 2.6 million employees

---

66 AVIVA (2019) 'Millions of Mid-Life Employees Expected To Quit Jobs To Provide Care' (press release). www.aviva.com/newsroom/news-releases/2019/10/millions-of-mid-life-employees-expected-to-quit-jobs-to-provide-care

aged forty-five and over expect that they will have to leave their jobs to care for a relative or partner – opting to personally take on care duties for their relatives as a means of minimising care bills. This decision, they say, is often coming at the expense of their career. Those in the so called 'sandwich generation' are also often on grandparenting duty as they try to help their children hold down a job.

Further:

- One in five (19%) employees aged forty-five and over in the UK expect to leave work to care for adult family members

- Women in particular (20%) are more likely to see their careers cut short by the need to care for a relative or a partner, but men are not far behind (17%)

- Just 6% of employers view caring pressures as a significant issue faced by their employees, highlighting a disconnect between employee and employer

These figures build on an already worrying figure from Carers UK: 2.6 million have already quit their job to care for a loved one who is older, disabled or seriously ill, with nearly half a million (468,000) leaving their job in the last two years alone – more than 600 people a day. This, they say, is a 12% increase since Carers

UK and YouGov polled the public in 2013.[67] Carers UK's findings also show that five million employees are juggling work with caring – a huge leap from the 2011 figure of three million, which, they say, 'emphasises the need for employers to support the rapidly increasing number of staff with caring responsibilities to stay in the workforce'.

This really hit home several years ago when I instituted a monthly session for each of the teams in my business: an hour or two when they had the chance (if they wished) to share something from their work and personal lives. Almost all of the older members of the team talked about the challenges they were facing balancing work with caring for elderly parents. The younger members of the team had been unaware, as had I. It lead me to have a series of fruitful conversations with my staff to see if they needed some slack in their working week to enable them to juggle their lives – one of the developments which converted me to the concept of an MLR.

Making flexible working happen

If you are going to have staff working away from the office on a regular basis, make sure they have the tools to do their job – laptops (or PCs if they need to run

---

67 Carers UK (2019) 'Research: More than 600 people quit work to look after older and disabled relatives every day', (press release). www.carersuk.org/news-and-campaigns/press-release-rss/6078-more-than-600-people-quit-work-to-look-after-older-and-disabled-relatives-every-day

demanding applications), secure access to your server, Skype, and so on. If you want to take the opportunity to build agile working practices into your company, now is the time you can integrate hot desking and office sharing into the equation. Staff can handle customer calls from home simply by ensuring they have a quiet room to work in, and if they are going to make video calls, a room with an appropriately bland background or company logo.

Theoretically, along with a happier (hopefully more motivated) workforce you can radically reduce your business occupational costs – as well as make your precious car parking spaces go further. The average allocation per employee has traditionally been 100 square feet. Combine the cost of rent, business rates, heating and so on and that can easily rack up to between £2,500 and £5,000 a year per employee – far more in prime London locations. If five people now occupy the space that four formerly did, which is a commonly used formula among property consultants now touting the merits of 'agile working', that's how much you can save.

The discussion around salary

One of the topics that has to be on the table if, following an MLR review, an employee elects to take on a less onerous role in the business, is salary. There can be an assumption that, because of their seniority or years with the business, they will carry on receiving (pro-rata) the same salary. That nettle needs to be grasped – not least because it limits your ability to remunerate the personnel replacing them, but it can severely disrupt your business dynamic if someone is seen to be receiving far more than another person doing the same job.

NINE

Reward And Benefit Structures

When was the last time you had a hard look at the way you reward and motivate your personnel? In particular, how you differentiate between people who are at various stages in their career – and their lives?

I'm not just talking about salary here, but the add-ons to their take-home pay that will not only motivate talented people to join your company, but to remain there as their needs and priorities evolve over time. What really mattered to someone who joined you from university could well have changed by forty-five as they start to look down the barrel of accumulating a decent pension over the next ten or twenty years.

The MLR is a terrific opportunity to bring the reward and benefit structure into the mix for an individual. It can be a matter of reprioritising the balance of what they receive, especially if you are looking to keep your staff costs neutral. Equally, there are some add-ons you might consider which, for a relatively modest amount of investment, can deliver a 'lot of bang for your buck'.

Pensions

One of the primary elements of any MLR is helping an employee understand precisely how they stand in regard to their future pension provision – not least because that information will help inform any decision they make on how long they need to continue working, whether or not they can afford to reduce their hours or change their role at some point, and whether they need to make an adjustment to the amount they are saving for their pension.

In the section of this book targeting employees we have spelled out the need for everyone (not just those in midlife) to take control of their financial future – including some of the statistics and figures included below, which highlight the need to make sure their pensions are in good shape.

Many people in their forties onwards will already have a good handle on where they stand, especially if your business makes a point of providing a detailed statement each year setting that out. Many, but not all. Statistics show that a worryingly high proportion of people are inclined to put off worrying about events that seem a long way into the future, while many more have major concerns about the future but aren't taking steps to address it. Others are simply struggling to cope with the pressures they are currently under.

Part of the problem is that people tend to wildly overestimate just how much they will receive from their pension pot. Financial services provider Sanlam UK has come to similar conclusions in their latest 'What's Your Number?' report – which found that more than half of UK adults doubt they'll be able to put away enough money to retire when they would like to.[68] Only 12% of under fifty-fives actually have a target for their pension pots, surely the one figure they should have front of mind – and even fewer (3%) know what their target pension pot should be to achieve financial security in retirement.

A 2019 report issued by the World Economic Forum which looked globally at the future of pensions says that retirees in the UK are, on average, likely to run out of all but their state pension 10.3 years before death, with women running out even earlier – at 12.6

---

68 Sanlam (2019) 'What's Your Number?' www.sanlam.co.uk/ document-repository / group-brochures / 2040-what-s-your-number-research-report

years.[69] The cause, they say, is increasing longevity which has not been matched by increases in savings for pensions.

The state pension can form a handy base for an individual's income in retirement, but it is currently around £9,000 a year. A recent *Which?* report[70] found that couples required around £27,000 a year (£20,000 for individuals) to cover all the basic areas of expenditure together with a few luxuries, such as holidays, hobbies and eating out. That rose to £42,000 a year for couples (£33,000 for an individual) if the odd long-haul holiday and car renewal every five years is included. Currently, the average amount that people have in their DC pot when they retire is just £61,897,[71] which would only yield a miserly £2,500 a year.

Hopefully, your employees are in better financial shape than that, but being armed with this data, employers can play a key role in encouraging their staff to reflect upon what sort of retirement they are aspiring to and where they stand in relation to achieving that. Even better, if you have a financial adviser or employees benefits company managing staff pensions, putting

---

69 Tom Bailey (2019) 'British pensioners are running out of money a decade too early', Moneywise. www.moneywise.co.uk/news/2019-06-17/british-pensioners-are-running-out-money-decade-too-early

70 Paul Davies (2019) 'How much will you need to retire?', Which?. www.which.co.uk/money/pensions-and-retirement/starting-to-plan-your-retirement/how-much-will-you-need-to-retire-atu0z9k0lw3p

71 Patrick Collinson (2019) 'Five figures that show why you should be worried about pensions', *The Guardian*. www.theguardian.com/money/2019/sep/28/uk-pensions-saving-retirement

them in front of each employee on a regular basis is one of the most responsible and helpful things you can do. They will be able to use an industry or proprietary calculation tool to explain exactly what their current pot will deliver against their expectations, and how much more they need to add to it in the years they plan to carry on working, either through contributions to their pension or into other investment vehicles such as ISAs.

This will provide vital background for any further discussions on their career and role. It's also worth considering that, while employees have the option to increase their contributions, employers also have the option to match that, and someone may well consider trading a future pay rise for a (tax-free) boost to their pension.

What happens at fifty-five?

Worth including in any discussion with an employee – especially if they can be provided with expert advice – is what an individual can do once they reach the age of fifty-five. The fifty-five benchmark really matters because this is when an individual is entitled to start taking up to 25% of its value out of a pension pot in cash, transferring it, and/or exchanging it for either a drawdown or annuity pension. This can be an opportunity for someone to adjust their work/life balance such as winding down or moving to a less onerous role, or even retiring or moving into self-employment or consultancy.

In the past, those on generous DB pensions were often encouraged to leave at this point by employers not too keen to see their pension liabilities continue to mount, as well as a pretext for allowing older employees to make room for thrusting young executives. DB pensions are fast becoming a thing of the past, but for those lucky enough to have built up a generous pension, there may well be more options for them to consider. There are risks attached though. Taking out up to 25% of a pension pot (the amount allowed before punitive tax rates set in) can have a major impact if the pot is small to start with. Equally, reinvesting it should only ever be done with expert guidance – especially if someone is considering transferring a DB into a DC one. The current transfer rates are generous and quite possibly tempting, but any potential downsides in terms of security should also be taken on board.

Other benefits

Bearing in mind their priorities, here are some benefits that you might consider discussing with someone in their forties and fifties upwards, especially as you or your employee benefit provider will often be able to negotiate better rates than they can.

Private medical insurance (PMI): older employees won't necessarily be more prone to ailments than their younger counterparts – in fact they tend to carry on through illnesses because of their inbuilt work ethic. PMI can provide considerable reassurance to both them and their employer, especially if it means they can be treated promptly and at a time of their choosing when ever-lengthening NHS waiting lists are a worry. Partners can also be included in policies if you want to go the extra mile and it can also extend to dental care.

Critical illness cover: this will normally cover strokes, heart attacks and non-terminal cancer, can be negotiated at far better rates by an employer, and would be seen as a positive incentive by an older employee keen to protect their partner or family.

Life insurance: this will also provide funds should the individual be diagnosed with a terminal illness and provide for a person's dependents at a vulnerable time.

Death in service benefit: this serves a similar purpose to life insurance, and usually provides between two and four times the annual salary should an individual die while employed by you, regardless of whether or not their demise was work-related.

Other employee health benefits: providing options to boost fitness and health, for instance, through gym membership, regular health checks, free eye and allergy tests, a dental plan or access to a chiropractor ties into any discussion on maintaining or improving an employee's wellbeing.

Employee discounts: if you want to enhance your employee's lifestyles at little cost to yourself, discount cards for use in retail outlets, supermarkets and leisure venues are readily available from as little as £50 a year.

Employee Assistance Programmes: these provide employees with telephone or Facetime access to health advice, including mental health – quicker and easier than trying to get an appointment with one's GP.

Buying holidays: fairly standard now for younger employees to request, but potentially a highly attractive possibility for older employees who would prefer to wind down a notch or two in the months and years ahead or if they have family care responsibilities.

TEN

Design and Delivery

If your business is considering implementing the MLR, how should you design and deliver it? Let's look at two of the largest pilots to date for any lessons that can be learned from them.

The Legal & General experience

Legal & General was one of the organisations that put its staff forward, along with Aviva, to be involved in the first wave of trials of the MLR. John Power, Strategic Development Director in their Retirement division, says that, for Legal & General, it was part of getting to understand their market better.

In John's words:

'At the time, we were looking at growing our share of the annuity market and saw this as an opportunity to learn from the mindsets of people pre-retirement. But you soon realise that a secure retirement income is just one small part of the equation.

The "Cridland Report" had opened up a whole series of issues to address, not least the sustainability of the state pension, whether the state pension age should change and so on. Yes, the Government wants people to work for longer, because they will rely less on state benefits. So how could we help people bridge the gap – possibly up to sixty-eight and beyond?

We started to think about what other parts of a good value conversation would help people to weigh up their current situation and reflect on their future. I myself was fifty at the time, so I looked at what I personally would want to take stock of over the next ten to fifteen years of my life. Could it be setting up my own business, volunteering, working part-time with a charity – any or all of these things?

But that's linked to my financial wellbeing – can my family and I afford for me to do these things? Health came into the equation too – if you haven't got your health your options are restricted. Getting involved in the MLR would help us see things in the round.

Aviva had already done some trials – looking at the three strands of health, wealth and work. We got involved and ran some concept testing. We readily found sixty people interested within Legal & General, aged forty-five to fifty-five, and ran four workshops in the South-East. We had the advantage of having our own pension planning tool, as well as a stake in a financial wellbeing company called Salary Finance (www.salaryfinance.com/uk).

What they brought to the party that was different was recognising that some people in this age group aren't only looking ahead to how they can afford to retire: they are also facing some financial problems now – debt, supporting their family, helping their children through university and so on.

That led to us harnessing the Salary Finance toolbox – differentiating pension planning from financial wellbeing by offering debt management support and tips, simple savings plans, and affordable loans linked to payroll.

And while I'd say our staff are pretty financially savvy, we recognised that if you were to roll out an offer like this to other companies, you could add in the element of financial education. One of the most interesting and positive pieces of feedback we received was that people said they wished they'd had access to that sort of advice fifteen years previously – and how they would work to get their kids to learn more about money management.

The workshops we ran each had fifteen people in them, and we broke them down into four sections:

- Pensions: am I on track to have the retirement income of my dreams?

- Financial wellbeing: do I need help with rainy day savings, day to day budgeting or debt management?

- Health: am I on track to be the healthiest me I can be?

- Career: how do I see myself spending the next ten/ fifteen years? What work/life balance do I seek?

Our own retirement planning tool was used with the first element, Salary Finance ran one element, and the health component was run by a specialist company called Road to Health (since acquired by Inchora) who used their Quealth app (www.quealth.co). This is a useful online resource where you put your health, fitness and lifestyle data in and it gives you a health risk assessment against the most common diseases and suggests the top five things you could do in the light of the results, plus some online coaching. We also had a couple of peripatetic nurses on hand to carry out basic health checks such as accurate height, weight and BMI measurements, blood pressure and cholesterol readings.

For the career component we partnered with Prospects Group who do a lot of work for the National Career Service (www.prospects.co.uk). They ran a group workshop to discuss the changing world of work and how everyone could think about the impacts on them and what they wanted to achieve from the next stage in their working lives.'

Which of the strands fared best?

'People were actually really keen to find out about their health, helped I think by the confidential health check with the nurse. Least successful, curiously, was the career element, with a far wider mix of feedback from participants with a number of people saying they didn't particularly feel they needed help in this area. However, this was a mixed group with our own HR bods as well as some senior people. That could easily have put people off, and I also think it being a group discussion rather than one-to-one didn't suit everyone either.

What did come across throughout all the sessions was that people did enjoy listening to other people's stories and learning from their experiences.'

What did we learn going forward from the way we ran these sessions?

'Firstly, that it is possible to harness digital tools to roll out reviews on a large scale, but advisers will be needed at several steps of the journey.

Secondly, employers – for a relatively modest investment – could and should make reviews available to their people. A great place to start would be to talk to you pension provider; can they help structure MLR sessions?

Thirdly, because of some people's concerns around confidentiality, you might need outside consultants – or at least access to a confidential ear – as part of the process. We are thinking about partnering with our union colleagues from Unite, who have around a dozen qualified "UnionLearn Representatives" who are trained by the Trades Union Congress to deliver midlife reviews and could act in this way. That said, if you are to have a meaningful conversation around careers, an individual's manager needs to be part of the discussion.

We also discovered that there were valuable insights when people used the opportunity to have a discussion with their partner too, and to involve them in the decision making.'

The Aviva experience

Alistair McQueen is Head of Savings and Retirement at Aviva. As well as playing a key role in testing out the pilot project with Aviva in 2017, he is now heading up the rollout of the concept across the entire company – the first to do so.

In Alistair's words:

'One of our biggest drivers at Aviva is pensions – and so helping people prepare for later life. But for us it's not just about the business. We feel we have a social responsibility as well. We also feel we have a voice around ageing and society and can help manage some of the processes of an ageing society. And there are two levers that people can pull to manage a longer life: they can save more and/or work for longer. We took inspiration from the Cridland Review of the SPA, who said it's one thing to crank up the SPA – but it's unfair to do that without supporting people to stay in work.

So, in 2018 we ran a pilot in one of our locations and invited 500 people to come along, aged forty-five plus; and while at the beginning it was seen as a nice-to-do altruistic gesture by our management, it soon led to an important mindset shift within Aviva. We designed our own review process, which evolved along the way. It was initially going to be a financial education piece, but when we spoke to our staff, they quickly said that their life was much more than just their money. It's about health and wellbeing too. And about career development.

So that's what we've created – an intervention that we call the Midlife MOT, helping people to consider their wealth, their wellbeing and their work. It turned into a relatively short intervention: two hours away from the desk to consider these three things. We managed expectations by telling participants that they weren't going to leave a session as a financial expert, career guru or wellbeing wizard!

The objective was to give personnel some confidence in their decisions, encourage them to pause for reflection and provide some awareness of what other levers they could pull on when they left the room. We had no idea what response we'd get – but we sent out an invitation and got a 94% take-up rate. That told us that there is an unsatisfied need for help among this demographic.

Aviva is a generous employer, but it was plain from this response that this particular demographic felt ignored. For instance, we've got training when you join the company and up to the age of forty-five, but once you reached forty-five plus (and it's not written down anywhere) the perception was that your career was on the wind down.

One in three of our older workers told us that they felt age was a barrier to career opportunities. Initially we thought two out of three thinking the opposite must be a good thing, but within this forty-five plus demographic Aviva has 5,000 people. So that means we have 1,500 people who feel age is holding them back. The other piece of feedback we got was that there is an unwritten understanding within the company that career development ends at fifty. Culturally we have created this mindset.

We took this to our management, thinking they'd say: "Come back when you have more evidence of outcomes. For instance, are they saving more? Investing more in their career development? Or getting fitter?" To their credit, they actually said that the demand to take part and staff's dissatisfaction with their development opportunities, together with an early indication of a boost in confidence was more than enough evidence. So, in 2019 we started taking it to all of our locations: we now have a national MOT service for all of our people aged forty-five plus, something we will undertake on an annual basis.'

How is the course structured?

'When people come into this, they instinctively assume that it's a pre-retirement course. We quickly have to let them know that it's actually an anti-retirement course. If the outcome of people doing our course is people retiring sooner, then we have failed.

We have three legs, and many people are up to speed on the finances, they will know a bit more than the average twenty-five year old would. But they haven't given any consideration towards career development for years. They won't know that the average healthy life expectancy is sixty-three[72] but they won't be getting the state pension until they are sixty-six, sixty-seven or even sixty-eight.

And when we ask them who they get advice from on this sort of subject, it's always "family" or "mum and dad". The danger is that the experience their older family members have had isn't necessarily going to be the one that they're going to have themselves. Their "Dad" had a job for life, bought his first house at twenty-five, paid his mortgage off at fifty, had a final salary pension and got a state pension at sixty-five. That's not their situation.

The work element has a considerable section on training and development, and we use case studies to showcase individuals and challenge their preconceived ideas. A classic example is that because Aviva is a large employer, it has to pay an apprenticeship levy to the Government. If we don't use it, we lose it. Instinctively people assume it's aimed at younger personnel, but we have a sixty-seven year old now

72 Office for National Statistics (2017) 'What affects an area's healthy life expectancy?'. www.ons. gov.uk/peoplepopulationandcommunity/ healthandsocialcare/healthandlifeexpectancies/articles/ whataffectsanareashealthylifeexpectancy/2018-01-18

doing an apprenticeship course. This is not just about youth. We showcase people who retrain and move jobs. We want to squash the idea that career development ends at fifty.

The work we've done on the MOT has also led to us developing more support for employees who are also carers – and everyone knows how many carers leave their jobs because they cannot combine both roles. That particular initiative started with one member of staff who had been looking after younger as well as older members of their family, and they had the passion and energy to say we needed to do more. He campaigned internally on the platform that – if we really are an employer for all ages, and where age is no barrier for opportunity – then we cannot ignore older staff with big caring responsibilities.

That resulted in the caring leave that we now provide, paid and unpaid, which matches that for staff caring for younger members of their family: thirty-five hours paid leave, thirty-five hours unpaid leave a year, plus the support of a carer's network within the organisation. We now celebrate this caring responsibility. And it's not just being altruistic. With the scarcity of talent coming through, if Aviva can project a perception that we are a caring employer, we will win this future war for talent.

It might sound like we have become a more flexible employer, but the policies were all in existence and known about at board level – some staff at lower levels just weren't aware of them. Now we take 5,000 people aside every year and say: "You have the right to ask for flexible working. You have the right to have a phased retirement. And you can tell your manager that."'

And the big difference Aviva that expects to make?

'The MOT pilot actually led to a radical rethink within the company, because only by going through this exercise did we unearth a huge business risk that Aviva was facing. One-third of our workforce is over the age of forty-five, the fastest growing demographic within the organisation, but we did not appreciate that until we undertook this exercise. We also have an incredibly loyal workforce – the average length of service of this particular demographic is seventeen years. That's 85,000 years of experience contained within that body of people. They know how to get things done, who to speak to, and how to speak to them. They are an essential asset to the wellbeing of our organisation.

We also realised that the rate at which they were leaving us was faster than the demographic beneath them: not just because they are coming up to retirement age, but because, within Aviva, this demographic has a high proportion of final salary pension wealth. This gives the power to the individual to choose when they leave. They might not need to carry on working, and the pressure is on us to look after them. So we had a huge asset that we were neglecting, and the business was facing a real risk in coming years – some core systems, core management processes that we would not be able to run because we didn't have the skills set.

That's when we shifted the MOT from being a "nice-to-do" to a "need-to-do". From a management perspective, it is now a retention tool. How can we retain these skills, make these people feel valued within the organisation? It's still being refined – and that's a core focus for us this year. Over the next few years we're going to have to put some heavy business metrics around it, focusing on retention, on productivity, absenteeism, recruitment. That's where the mindset is now within Aviva. For us the Midlife MOT is not just about altruism: it's also driven by our business objectives.'

Conclusion: Making The Midlife Review Work For You

The biggest single message that comes out of all the research to date, and from the pilot schemes, is that there is no 'one size fits all'. Companies should first consider looking at the elements that have worked well elsewhere and then create a template that functions best for them.

Testing that template with a smaller group of personnel before rolling it out company-wide is also a sensible route to take. This will be especially important for SMEs who may not have the resources available to try out models that have so far only been used by larger corporates.

According to the Centre for Ageing Better in their September 2019 report, 'Developing the Midlife

MOT', the concept is still in the early stages and the organisations who have so far piloted the concept are still developing their offer for future iterations. They advise that any organisation considering developing their own MLR consider the following:

- Know your target audience – consider the purpose and intended outcomes.

- 'Age' is not a fixed concept – consider what age you are targeting the service for.

- There is no 'one size fits all' for delivery – whether by telephone consultations, face-to-face, group sessions or online tools, consider what format is most applicable and effective for the intended participant group.

- Keep the content focused – an MLR can't cover everything; prioritisation in content is important to maintain focus, clarity of purpose, and participant engagement.

- The MLR is a process, not a one-off event – practical outputs, signposting and follow-ups are required to engage and benefit participants.

- When you look at the broad sweep of the MLR – taking in wealth, health and work – it may well be advisable to bring in outside consultants or advisers for some elements, or harnessing what specialisms you already have to hand. If you already use employee benefits specialists, they will be able to undertake the wealth aspects of an

MLR – ditto financial advisers if they currently help you plan your pensions.

Both can operate at different levels such as telephone advice, group sessions or one-to-one advice, offering you a variety of outlays as well as granularity in the information they can impart. Discussing someone's career aspirations and options might well be handled by an internal HR department but if you are looking to build trust with staff who might harbour anxieties about the motives behind an MLR, using an outside HR specialist (at least in the initial stages) might well prove an investment.

If you would like to discuss what the MLR could do for your company, Punter Southall Aspire has established an MLR platform where companies can provide employees access to content and tools to support their forty-five plus employees through the second half of their career and into retirement and input on getting this important concepts off the ground in the UK.

Resources

Pension Wise: a free and impartial government guidance about your defined contribution pension options (www.pensionwise.gov.uk)

State Pension Forecast: find out when you will be entitled to receive your state pension and how much it will be (www.gov.uk/check-state-pension)

The Money and Pension Service: arms-length body sponsored by the DWP helping people make the most of their pensions and savings (www.moneyandpensionsservice.org.uk)

The Pensions Advisory Service: providing free, independent and impartial information and guidance about pensions to members of the public (www.pensionsadvisoryservice.org.uk)

Pension Credit: a safety net if you aren't entitled to a full New State Pension and you have no other income (www.gov.uk/pension-credit)

Pension Tracing Service: free Government service helping to reconnect you to pension post from previous employer (www.findpensioncontacts.service.gov.uk)

My Lost Account: free service which allows you to you search for accounts with thirty banks, forty-three building societies and NS&I (www.mylostaccount.org.uk)

Unclaimed Assets Register: service run by Experian which will charge you a small fee for helping you reclaim lost savings and investments (www.uar.co.uk)

National Careers Service: information: advice and guidance to help you make decisions on learning, training and work (nationalcareers.service.gov.uk)

NHS Health Check: a free health check-up for adults in England aged forty to seventy-four (www.nhs.uk/conditions/nhs-health-check)

Business in the Community: the oldest and largest business-led membership organisation dedicated to responsible business (www.bitc.org.uk)

Punter Southall Aspire: a major financial planning and retirement savings business, advising SMEs on how to transform their personnel's financial future (www.psaspire.com)

National Institute of Adult Continuing Education: an organisation that aims to encourages more and different adults to engage in learning of all kinds (www.local.gov.uk/our-support/research/partner-organisations/national-institute-adult-continuing-education-niace)

The Centre for Ageing Better: a Lottery-funded research body working to create a society where everyone enjoys a good later life (www.ageing-better.org.uk)

Tim Drake (2017) *Generation Cherry: Powerful strategies to give you a second bite of the cherry.* (Brentford: Reddoor Publishing.)

Shurety Coaching: business and health coaching specialists (www.shuretycoaching.com)

Positive Ageing Coaching: life coaching and forthcoming book on managing personal change (www.positiveageingcoaching.com)

Renegade Generation: a company helping individuals reassess their career options and providing ageing workforce solutions to employers (www.renegadegeneration.com)

LKWC Ltd: specialists in learning and careers (www.midlifecareers.co.uk)

Prolis: Midlife Review Consulting (www.prolis.co.uk)

The Authors

Steve Butler

Steve Butler is a Chartered Manager and Fellow of the Chartered Management Institute. He gained his Master's in Business Administration from Solent University and is currently researching for his Doctorate in Business Administration at Winchester University. He is a regular writer and speaker on inter-generational working, retirement and older worker business management issues. He is also passionate about helping corporates and individuals become more financially informed.

Steve is Chief Executive of Punter Southall Aspire, a national retirement savings business with 150 employees building a range of solutions including corporate employee benefit consulting, face-to-face financial planning advice, telephone and online retirement guidance and advice, supported by innovative technology systems with the ambition to transform people's financial future.

He has recently turned fifty, leading him to reflect on what the next twenty years of his own working life could look like, and how he can proactively manage his wealth, health and career to achieve these new ambitions.

Tony Watts OBE

Tony is a freelance writer, journalist and commentator who has spent over thirty years writing about later life issues as well as a range of other business topics. He helped set up and edited the UK's first national newspaper for older people and has written a number of books on the subject. In his voluntary time, he also represents older people regionally and nationally and campaigns on their behalf. He was awarded an OBE in 2014 for his work on behalf of older people.

Printed in Great Britain
by Amazon